I Want Happiness NOW!

I Want Happiness NOW!

Dr. Henry Brandt
with Phil Landrum

ZONDERVAN PUBLISHING HOUSE

OF THE ZONDERVAN CORPORATION | GRAND RAPIDS, MICHIGAN 49506

I WANT HAPPINESS NOW
Copyright © 1978 by Henry Brandt
Grand Rapids, Michigan

Library of Congress Cataloging in Publication Data

Brandt, Henry R
   I want happiness now!
   1. Christian life—1960-   I. Landrum, Phil, joint author. II. Title.
BV4501.2.B686   248'.4   78-14510

ISBN 0-310-21641-9

All Scripture references are taken from the *New American Standard Bible.* Copyright 1960, 1962, 1968, 1971, 1972 by The Lockman Foundation. Used by permission.

Printed in the United States of America

83   84   85   86   87   88 — 10 9 8 7 6

Preface

Preface

It has been my privilege to be a professional counselor for thirty years. I've consulted with lawyers, doctors, dentists, businessmen, tradesmen, executives, factory workers, laborers, waiters and waitresses, janitors, the unemployed, the rich and the poor, the educated and the uneducated, the brilliant and the dull, those from good homes and those from miserable homes, males and females.

All these people have one thing in common: they come in to find relief for their desperately unhappy, frustrated, hopeless condition resulting from their response to the conditions and people in their world.

Frequently, these people face conditions that cannot be reversed—being fired from their jobs, bankruptcy, poverty, broken marriages, miserable home conditions, mean people, rejection, maimed bodies, the death of a key person in their lives.

If these people have any hope for restoring or finding contentment, it must happen within themselves. It has been my joy and satisfaction to observe thousands of dejected, desperately unhappy people turn into radiant, contented, happy persons as they opened themselves to the resources of God alone who died that we might live. As the Psalmist has said:

> Oh give thanks unto the LORD, for He is good; For His lovingkindness is everlasting. For He has satisfied the thirsty soul, and the hungry soul He has filled with what is good (Ps. 107:1,9).

The process involved in tapping the resources freely given to us by God is what this book is all about.

1 / The Indestructibles

1 / The Indestructibles

WHY ARE SOME PEOPLE ALWAYS HAPPY? /

A line of research concerning a group of young people called "indestructibles" was reported recently in a leading psychological journal.

These indestructibles lived under extreme poverty, and came from very bad home conditions which were located in slum neighborhoods.

Yet, they were well adjusted and good students.

The researchers wondered if we haven't erred in the past by studying maladjusted people in order to draw conclusions about good self-images. Why not study well-adjusted people instead?

That question got me to thinking of some people I've met in my life who fit the description of indestructibles.

It is true that we cannot prevent troublesome or sorrowful events from intruding into our lives. But some people live heartily, joyfully, considerately one day at a time. They rely on their power of choice, whether their problems are solved today or not.

PHYLLIS AND JIM AREN'T WORRIED /

I recently saw Phyllis and Jim weather a storm that would destroy most people.

They had been married sixteen years, and had three children—ages fifteen, thirteen, and ten. The family often did things together . . . hiking, playing tennis, boating, attending church, entertaining friends, skiing.

In the home, Phyllis had her duties and Jim had his.

She was proud of his progress on his job and his civic and church activities.

He admired the way she kept house, managed the family, got along with her friends.

THEN IT HAPPENED! /

Then, without any advance warning, the company Jim worked for suddenly ceased operating.

Just . . . sudden unemployment . . . at a time when they were building a new house. Yet, there was no panic.

Phyllis trimmed the food budget, and reassured Jim that she was trusting God to help them in this crisis.

They prayed together and patiently waited as Jim looked for another job. They used his free time for family fun—inexpensive activities, of course.

They went on picnics in the park, hiked over trails, played tennis at the public courts, went bicycling.

Jim reassured Phyllis that he wasn't afraid—or worried. His faith was in God, and he was enjoying this time of watching an uncertain future unravel.

In a few months, he found another job.

Phyllis and Jim look back on that period as one of the best of their lives.

They are among the indestructibles. They had a faith and hope that enabled them to live above their depressing circumstances.

Now, meet another indestructible.

MEMORIES OF A DITCHDIGGER /

He was one of our next-door neighbors when I was a teen-ager. It was during those turbulent years between 1930 and 1933—the height of the Depression.

People by the droves were out of work; they were losing their life savings as a result of bank failures and were being evicted from their homes. Suicides were frequent. Nervous breakdowns were common.

Strangely enough, the depression years were happy, positive, relaxed ones for me, partially because of that next-door neighbor.

He was a highly skilled (and highly paid) tool-and-die-maker. Suddenly, he was without a job or a pay-check.

The best he could do was get a job with the WPA, a governmental agency which gave menial jobs to as many people as possible.

His assignment: dig ditches.

WE WERE SHOCKED /

This seemed a terrible thing to me. Imagine this top-flight craftsman digging ditches!

Without complaining, he went to his job every day. At night he returned, his attitude as positive as if he had his old job.

We had a big front porch on our house, and many nights the people from the neighborhood would gather on our porch. This man was one of them.

One night he got to talking enthusiastically about the fine art of digging ditches and how he was enjoying the opportunity of working outdoors and using his strength to accomplish a task.

"I've never felt better in my life," he commented.

WE VISIT THE WORK DETAIL /

We boys were so fascinated by his enthusiasm that we went to watch him. Most of the men who worked with him were leaning on their shovels, looking miserable.

Not our neighbor.

When he saw us, he stopped to take us on a quick tour. He told us how to dig a ditch. Then he showed us his handiwork. His ditches were straight . . . uniformly deep—with firm sides.

"Aren't they beautiful?" He was proud of his ditches.

EVENINGS ON THE PORCH /

Another night "our group" was sitting on the porch, watching the sun go down. The sunset was beautiful, and this neighbor was overtaken with enthusiasm.

I mean really excited! About a sunset.

"What a beautiful sunset!" he exclaimed. "What a miracle to watch!" Even though he had experienced a letdown that would have depressed many, he could get excited about a sunset.

A PROMOTION /

One night, he announced that he had been made foreman. He was filled with compassion and pity for his men. They refused to accept their lot in life and spent the day moaning and complaining.

Our neighbor now had a new zest for his job—the challenge of lifting his men out of despondency and showing them how to be thankful they had some work to do.

HE HAD LEARNED AN IMPORTANT LESSON /

As I watched this highly skilled craftsman who could find a challenge and satisfaction in anything he did, I realized he had mastered a pivotal principle: it was not the task that was important, but the spirit he brought to that task.

He brought an undaunted spirit to every task and experience. As a result, he was happy and successful.

GARDEN DAYS /

The next spring he made a garden. He was equally thrilled with the garden and worked in it every evening. The entire process fascinated him.

"What a miracle," he would say. "Look at everything grow." To others, a garden was so much dust, mud, and hours of bending over. To my neighbor, it was a miracle.

This man had a faith that sustained him. His faith could be summed up in this paragraph from the Bible:

> Trust in the LORD with all your heart, and do not lean on your own understanding. In all your ways acknowledge Him, and He will make your paths straight (Prov. 3:5-6).

OTHER INDESTRUCTIBLES /

There were other men in the neighborhood who lived by the same faith. Many nights the conversation on our front porch turned to what to do about unpaid taxes, unpaid bills, postponed car repairs or house repairs, because there was no money.

They would talk about someone who had had his car repossessed or who had lost a home, or about standing in line for welfare checks. Frequently, they would pray together, expressing their faith in a guiding God, asking Him to comfort their friends.

They prayed for each other, too, reaffirming their own faith and asking God for peace and wisdom.

Those prayers seemed to settle everything— nothing to worry about. Everything was in God's hands. At least, that's the way it seemed to me.

A NEIGHBORHOOD PROJECT /

One night one of the men suggested: "We don't have any money, but we've got lots of energy. Let's build a tennis court." Men and boys together built a clay court.

I spent many hours pulling a heavy roller. Others used rakes, hoes, shovels. After many weeks, we were done. What a day—when the men and the boys lined up and looked at the brand new lines made of white lime.

Weren't we proud!

We spent many happy hours playing tennis on the court made by our own hands.

These were men of faith. They didn't know what their future held for them. But they trusted their God. These people were indestructibles. They had an optimism and a hope that carried them past the Depression, through World War II, the Korean War, various recessions since then, past the Vietnam War, and through the Energy crisis.

ANOTHER CRISIS /

My neighbor, the toolmaker, had another difficult experience to weather about ten years ago. He was working for a firm that went bankrupt. In one day, he had to face up to two hard facts: his job was gone and so was the retirement plan he had contributed to for twenty years.

He met this problem with the same faith he had shown in front of us back in the 30s. Other neighbors have faced many difficult problems since, but their faith and hope did not rest on changeable circumstances or the mistakes of other people. They also were among the indestructibles. Their source of faith and hope could best be described by another Bible quotation:

> . . . for I have learned to be content in whatever circumstances I am. I know how to get along with humble means, and I also know how to live in prosperity . . . In any and every circumstance I have learned the secret of being filled and going hungry, both of having abundance and suffering need (Phil. 4:11-12).

My family and some of my neighbors had found that secret.

MANY PEOPLE HAVEN'T /

Many of my neighbors during the Depression were not indestructible.

One of my playmates would come running breathlessly over to our house about once a week. His mother and father were drunk again, and were beating each other.

His dad would break furniture and throw pots and pans through the window. No one could help them because they were so bitter. Their lives and property were in shambles.

Another playmate had a mother who would sit all day, stare out of the window, and cry. Her husband had run away. No one knew where he was. There were many such stories.

In my early teens I saw people respond in different ways to the same circumstances.

HOW DO YOU BECOME AN INDESTRUCTIBLE? /

How do you join the ranks of those unusual people who are contented no matter what their situation is?

How can you have a great time on a "rotten" vacation? How do you enjoy life in the face of a financial failure, a negligent husband, an unresponsive wife, job setbacks?

Or . . . even how do you cope with success?

How do you handle maddening daily schedules? Little, everyday irritants? A room full of screaming children?

Also, how do you handle the lonely moments or decisions when no one stands with you—not even your family and friends?

In other words: how can you find contentment—right now?

There is a way.

2 / Chasing Rainbows

2 / Chasing Rainbows

IN SEARCH OF THE GOLDEN POT /

> I have learned to be content in whatever circumstances I am (Phil. 4:11).

We tend to chase that golden pot at the end of the rainbow, that something *in the future* that will bring us contentment.

Hopefully, some new experience, some new success, some new degree of cooperation or obedience from the people around us, or meeting someone new.

We have all listened to someone wistfully say:

"If I could only get that promotion, then I would be happy. . . ."

"Being a housewife is degrading. If only I had a job. . . ."

"If my husband would only pay more attention to me, then I would be. . . ."

"If only our children would obey, then we'd. . . ."

A NEW DAY /

I've listened to many people describe their hopes with excitement in their voices, their eyes sparkle, and happy smiles light up their faces. Generally, such optimism consumes us when there are prospects for something new in the future:

"I'm getting married."

"I'm starting a new job."

"I made a wonderful investment."

"We are building a new house."

"We are expecting a baby."
"I've made a fortune."
"We are taking a trip."
"I'm going to college."

TURNED TO ASHES . . . /

I've listened to the same people who have been in pursuit of something new for a while—perhaps years. Their hopes have turned to ashes. As they recount what happened, their eyes are slits, the corners of their mouths are turned down. Their voices tremble:

"My wife drives me nuts."
"My boss is unmerciful."
"My investment went sour."
"We have all kinds of problems with our new house."
"The baby bawls all night."
"My business drives me crazy."
"Our trip was awful."
"I hate college."

We all know people—perhaps our own children, parents, or close friends—who have spent many years in pursuit of education, wealth, power, social life, religious life.

Their goal was a fulfilled, contented, productive life. But they ended up depressed, sour, bitter, frustrated, empty, with broken friendships and marriages. They didn't learn "to be content in whatever circumstance they were."

A SHATTERED MARRIAGE /

The tragedy of seeking contentment out of human relationships is illustrated by Molly and Allan.

They started their marriage with the highest of hopes. Molly had been a very lonely, unhappy person who had fled from an unhappy home and was living alone.

Allan came from a home broken by a divorce. He was an independent person who did as he pleased. Molly liked his happy-go-lucky manner.

A WHIRLWIND COURTSHIP /

Their courtship was brief—a few months of whirlwind dating—then marriage and a happy life together (they thought).

It took only a few months for them to discover that marriage hadn't changed either one of them. Allan continued his independent ways, going and coming as he pleased—just being himself. Maybe he came home straight from work, maybe not.

When he didn't, he was confronted by a predictably cold, untouchable, angry woman. After listening to her tirades for a while, he would become increasingly disgusted and end up leaving the house, shouting at her.

The stuck it out for eleven long, miserable years—with Molly griping and complaining all the way. Allan just ignored her and continued to go his own way.

Finally, Allan announced that he was moving out, leaving the two children for Molly to worry about. Soon, he moved in with a girl friend.

As Molly told me her story, it was obvious that she was desperate. Her hands doubled into fists. Her voice shrilled. The tensed muscles in her face distorted her good looks.

"He comes home once a week to see the children," she told me. We have a boy, age nine, and a girl almost eleven. All week long I have to fuss with those kids. Then on the weekend, here comes Allan. He's relaxed, smug, and happy. It really burns me up."

If Allan is relaxed when he comes, it doesn't last long. Molly furiously berates him with all the hostile words she can think of.

"EACH WEEK IS LIKE WAR" /

Each visit ends the same way. Allan finally blows up. The two of them start shouting at each other, even hitting each other.

"Every week is like a war," she told me. "I don't know what to do. I don't want a divorce. I want my marriage back. But I can't stand the sight of that man."

By now, I suppose you have already taken sides and perhaps wonder where I stand.

ERROR-FILLED LOGIC /

Obviously, Allan is doing wrong. Even in our permissive society, very few people would condone his living arrangement with his girl friend—especially when he is still married to Molly. The Bible is crystal clear on this:

> You shall not commit adultery (Deut. 5:18)

But Allan insists that his wife's behavior is driving him into his girl friend's arms. Because he says it, however, doesn't make it true. He is clearly wrong.

When Molly storms around the house filled with tension, hostility, bitterness, and hatred, she surely isn't hurting Allan or his girl friend. They aren't there. She is alone, hurting only herself.

All this is going on underneath her own skin.

Molly insists that Allan causes her condition. If he would shape up, she would be a pleasant, responsive, happy woman. Because she says it so fervently, however, doesn't make her right. She also is wrong.

TWO PROBLEMS /

Allan and Molly had two problems, not one.

1. What to do about the marriage.
2. What to do about themselves.

Before anything could be done about the marriage, they had to do something about themselves. Allan refused to come to me for counseling, but Molly came back.

THE BAD NEWS /

"Tell me how to find contentment in this mess," she pleaded.

She needed some instruction. So together, we took a look at some Bible verses.

> The deeds of the flesh are evident, which are: immorality, impurity, sensuality, idolatry, sorcery, enmities, strife, jealousy, outbursts of anger, disputes, dissensions, factions, envyings, drunkenness, carousings, and things like these . . . (Gal. 5:19-21).

"Deeds of the flesh" come from within. Other people may give occasion for you to express them, but people don't cause them.

Which of these apply to Molly? Enmity, strife, jealousy, outbursts of anger, disputes, dissensions.

"What about Allan?" she shouted. "He's a lying, two-faced adulterer and blames me for driving him into that woman's arms."

True. Which of these apply to Allan? Immorality, sensuality, enmities, strife, outbursts of anger, disputes, dissensions.

If both Allan and Molly had a cold, each would need to be treated for his or her own cold. Likewise, each needed to deal with his or her own works of the flesh.

THE GOOD NEWS /

> But the fruit of the Spirit is love, joy, peace, patience, kindness, goodness, faithfulness, gentleness, self-control: against such things there is no law (Gal. 5:22-23).

What a relief it would be for Molly to be filled with such a Spirit. Especially when she was alone. Also, especially toward Allan.

"Why should I treat him like that?" she grumbled. "He doesn't deserve it."

True. He didn't. But why should his presence ruin her inner life and spoil her evenings?

Molly was noncommittal when she left. Isn't it strange how readily we accept and defend our outbursts of anger, disputes, and strife; and how steadfastly we resist love, joy, peace, and the rest of the fruit of the Spirit?

I've learned from my clients that the one who is mistreated tends to be preoccupied with the misdeeds of the offending one, but tends to justify personal negative behavior or reactions toward the offending person, even at the cost of personal misery.

The next time Molly came, I hardly recognized her. Her face was relaxed, the shrillness was gone from her voice. She was beautiful and content.

What had happened?

She had repented of her nastiness and had asked

God to give her His spiritual qualities. She had dealt with herself.

"Now, do you still want to work on saving your marriage?" I asked. She said she did.

HOW SHE SAVED HER MARRIAGE /

"Then, the next time Allan comes over, melt into his arms and give him a kiss such as you have never given him before." Her response to that was:

"Ugh."

"But let me warn you," I went on. "Don't be surprised if he doesn't respond."

Sure enough, the next time Allan showed up, she melted into his arms, and he got out of there and drove off.

He didn't know how to handle such behavior and fled, wondering what she was up to.

HAPPY ENDING /

There is a happy ending to this story. Molly had her lapses, but she continued to ask God to fill her with His qualities.

Allan's visits became mutually pleasant experiences. He wanted to find what Molly had found. He asked her to explain the basis for the change in her.

Molly simply explained that she had become so preoccupied with Allan's misdeeds that she had become totally blind to her own.

When it dawned on her that her nastiness was her own doing, she confessed the fact to the Lord, asked Him to forgive her, to cleanse her, and to strengthen her with His Spirit. When she saw clearly that she had been blaming Allan for her choices, by an act of her own will she took responsibility for her choices.

"I WAS WRONG" /

"I was very wrong in the way I treated you, Allan," she said. "And I'm sorry. Please forgive me, and with God's help I mean to respond to you as a wife should. What you do in relation to God is your choice."

He went away convinced that Molly was laying a trap. Now, when Allan came over, he was looking for a fight. She took months of mistreatment in exchange for her friendly, quiet manner.

Finally, he was convinced that the new Molly had something, and one day, all alone, he asked Jesus to invade his life, forgive him for his adulterous, nasty, selfish ways and give him the Spirit Molly had.

Today, nearly three years later, they are united as a family. They found the key to contentment.

They found that peace and love come from God, not from human relationships.

If they continue to turn Godward for the qualities that only He can give—love, joy, peace, patience, kindness, goodness, faithfulness, gentleness, self-control—they will become two indestructibles.

EMPTY SUCCESS /

Jim and Betty illustrate the futility of seeking contentment through financial success and accomplishments.

Jim is a big, strong, brilliant, talented man. His wife is an energetic, personable, competent lady.

He moved from extreme poverty as a child to reach a boyhood dream of owning his own business and becoming financially independent.

JUST A MODEST BUSINESS . . . /

They lived in California, not far from Yosemite National Park, and started renting trailers to people who wanted to haul their camping gear up the mountain.

It was a family business. Together, Jim and Betty installed hitches on the back bumpers of cars, hooked up trailers, and watched families happily head for Yosemite. The playground for their small children was the trailer lot, which was also the front yard of their house.

Their customers began asking if an ice box couldn't be installed in their trailers. Then they wanted an ice box and a cupboard. Then a tent trailer. Every change added weight to the trailers until they were so heavy the cars heated up when they pulled them up the mountain.

If only he could eliminate the car. Jim was a dreamer, an innovator, a pioneer. He started working on plans to produce a motor home that could be sold for half the price of current models.

For fourteen years Jim poured his entire life into the challenge of developing a motor-driven recreational vehicle. A company agreed to produce it, and quickly this motor-home company was outproducing and outselling all the competitors in the U.S.

Jim's dream was coming true. An industry-changing concept—a success story.

And . . . at the center of the dream was the main fact: financial success.

Jim and Betty were not people with *only* a dollar in mind.

One employee needed an operation and they paid the bill. They helped several employees with downpayments on their homes.

Another employee was confined to a wheelchair, but Jim hired him to wait on customers.

"He was a capable person, so why not?" Jim told me. "His appearance might have cost us a few sales, but his personality and efficiency gained us others."

Jim even arranged to have a special room built onto this man's house, designed to make life as comfortable as possible for him.

So, Jim was a nice guy, wasn't he? He was pleased because his idea made a contribution to making life more pleasant for American families. How often does a person have a chance to make that kind of contribution to our nation's main unit—the family?

He ultimately walked away from the effort with several million dollars.

He'd done it.

Now he could take it easy the rest of his life. It was just a matter of picking the place to retire.

Jim and Betty's search ended when they chose a plush condominium on one of Florida's choicest oceanfront sites.

"All my life I figured contentment would come when I reached this level in life," he said. "Now I could almost taste it."

"LET'S GO TO NASSAU FOR A HAMBURGER" /

Jim and his family arrived in Florida—ready to enjoy life fully. They accumulated the obligatory Cadillac, a fishing boat, a twin-engine plane.

So, Jim started into the good life. One day he would play golf. The next morning, walk the beach. Then jump in the plane and fly over to Nassau for a hamburger. Then come back and play tennis.

There was scuba diving, and deep-sea fishing for the big ones.

If Jim and his family got bored with southern Florida, they could whip back to California to Betty's parents' home (all 5,000 square feet of it) nestled on twenty acres, replete with fruit trees.

While they were there, the family could use their five dirt motorbikes and go hill climbing.

If the U.S. didn't present enough excitement, they could take off for Mexico . . . Alaska . . . South America . . . Europe . . . the world. And they did.

Quite a change of life for a boy who was born at the tail end of the Depression and didn't have enough money to even buy shoes for school.

He'd made it. And big.

Or had he?

"No. I hadn't. I had expected contentment to come with a better job . . . more money . . . the ultimate life. But after a few months of nonstop golf, tennis, and walking the beach, I found it wasn't true.

"I was completely empty."

You don't believe it, do you? "Aw, come on," is what you're saying to yourself. Right? How could Jim and Betty have an empty life with all those advantages?

But, it's true.

Even though Jim was an American success story and Mr. Nice Guy when it came to consideration for his fellow man . . . still, he was empty.

Isn't it strange? After fourteen years of hard work—intent upon reaching a goal, doing good things for fellow men along the way—he was now free to do anything his heart desired. And what did he find?

Emptiness.

Betty was by his side all the way. She, too, had the rug pulled out from under her. Many of her hopes for her family turned to ashes. There were strained relations between her and Jim.

I have walked along the beautiful Florida beaches with Betty and Jim, listening to their story of emptiness and hopelessness.

What, or where, is the key to contentment? For Betty and Jim, hard work, success, and wealth had led to an *empty pot* at the end of the rainbow.

ANOTHER HAPPY ENDING ... /

There is a happy ending.

They came to realize that enmity, strife, jealousy, outbursts of anger, disputes, and dissension were robbing them of the good life they had worked so hard to find.

The simple solution that worked for Molly and Allan also worked for them—confession, repentance, receiving forgiveness and cleansing, and also allowing God to strengthen them day by day.

The change in their lives has been incredible.

The husband-wife tension has slipped away. Family problems continue but no longer tear up their world. They don't have to travel around the world to find contentment. They discovered the basic truth that contentment isn't dependent on people or circumstances.

It comes from a person's relationship with God.

Let the apostle Paul say it:

> But though our outer man is decaying, yet our inner man is being renewed day by day (2 Cor. 4:16).

If they continue to turn Godward for the qualities that only God can give—love, joy, peace, patience, kindness, goodness, faithfulness, gentleness, self-control—they will become two *indestructibles*.

3 / Want Contentment? Make a Commitment!

3 / Want Contentment? Make a Commitment!

EVERYONE SEEKS CONTENTMENT /

Almost everyone who comes to my consulting room has been in pursuit of the advantages of life, but something or someone went wrong.

Their contentment and sense of self-worth or self-respect has been shattered. If self-respect and self-worth is intact, then the loss of contentment is attributed to the behavior of the offending person or to the circumstances that have shifted to one's disadvantage.

PLAYING THE ADVANTAGES-DISADVANTAGES GAME? /

Let me list some of the advantages we may be chasing and some of the disadvantages we are trying to eliminate.

Advantages	Disadvantages
education	lack of education
wealth	poverty
authority	no authority
high position	low position
beauty	plain
fame	unknown
popularity	unpopular
health	sick
marriage	singleness
singleness	marriage
retirement plan	no retirement plan

My clients tell me that advantages (or overcoming

the disadvantages) do not lead to contentment, joy, peace, or a sense of self-worth and self-respect.

We watch the lives of the famous and the popular end in misery. The same goes for the healthy, the educated, the rich, the powerful.

It's a frustrating world. Mechanical failures, impolite and careless people, social errors, noisy children, misunderstandings, and poor planning seem to make us angry—in spite of advantages.

Some years ago, a nationally respected head of the family relations department of a university put a bullet through his head. He was educated but miserable.

SEPARATE CARS /

One couple came to consult with me in separate cars because they couldn't stand to be in the same car together. One car was a Cadillac, the other a Mercedes.

They lived in a professionally decorated, color-coordinated house. They had unlimited wealth but couldn't purchase friendship.

Another client had responsibility for several thousand employees. He had plenty of power but he couldn't command tension and bitterness to leave his body.

THE GAME PRODUCES LOSERS /

By now you get my point. Surely, anyone would prefer to be educated, wealthy, powerful, and contented rather than uneducated, poor, powerless, and contented.

Nothing against advantages, you understand. But it is clear that advantages are just that—advantages. They, in themselves, do not produce contentment, joy, peace, a sense of self-worth or self-respect. If you play the advantages-disadvantages game, you'll always come up a loser.

That's quite a statement. If advantages don't produce these inner qualities, what does?

How can you be a Christian *and* be contented? How can you be famous *and* happy? Rich *and* at peace with yourself? Single *and* content? Married *and* happy? Poor *and* still enthusiastic about life? No beauty queen, *yet* with a good self-image?

There is an answer.

The next few pages may be a bit heavy reading, but they will launch us into finding the key to contentment. Jesus gives us the key in a reply to a question put to Him by a lawyer who asked:

> Teacher, which is the great commandment in the Law? And He said to him: "You shall love the Lord your God with all your heart, and with all your soul, and with all your mind. This is the great and foremost commandment. And a second is like it. You shall love your neighbor as yourself" (Matt. 22:36-39).

THREE STEPS TO CONTENTMENT /

This is a surprise answer to me. The key to contentment, then, boils down to this:

1. Love God
2. Love your neighbor
3. Love yourself

In modern language, Jesus is saying that a good self-image is based on self-respect, on loving your neighbor, and on loving God.

In presenting this idea to my clients, it leaves them cold and unresponsive at first glance. Doesn't contentment involve making enough money, getting an education, popularity, being understood, an understanding and decent marriage partner, obedient children, appreciative friends?

Your answer depends on whether you decide if Jesus knows what He is talking about. As for me, if Jesus said it, there is no need for a survey or a research project to verify His statements.

Like my clients, your answer will not be changed by a further statement on my part that I have seen thousands of changed lives verifying Christ's statements.

The only way for you to evaluate His advice is to take a step of faith and prove it to yourself. Take Him at His Word and launch out on your own quest to prove the truth of what He says. If you do, then commit a year, or two—or better yet, five years—to finding out.

STEP 1: LOVING GOD /

Assuming that you choose to take a step of faith, to make a commitment, come what may, let us proceed to step 1. Jesus said:

> You shall love the Lord your God with all your heart, and with all your soul, and with all your mind (Matt. 22:37).

What does this mean? You commit yourself to falling in love with Jesus. You give your quest all you've got.

HOW TO LOVE GOD /

How do you know if you love the Lord your God with all your heart, and with all your soul, and with all your mind? One of Jesus' disciples asked Him that question. Jesus' answer:

> He who has My commandments and keeps them, he it is who loves Me . . . (John 14:21).

To know His commandments is no easy process. They are contained in a big, thick book called the Bible. To become familiar with His commandments means long hours of study and application. To dig into that book is not a very exciting prospect at first glance. Is it worth it? Why should you take Jesus and His commandments seriously? Let Him speak for Himself. He said to His disciples:

> These things have I spoken to you, that in Me you may have peace . . . (John 16:33).
>
> . . . that your joy may be full (John 15:11).
>
> . . . .that you may be kept from stumbling (Jude 24).

Israel's King David, one of the wisest men who ever lived, offers this advice:

> How blessed is the man who(se) . . . delight is in the law of the Lord, and in His law he meditates day and night (Ps. 1:1-2).

These are beautiful promises.

A STEP OF FAITH /

Surely some of my readers have taken a stab at reading the Bible, only to find it to be a dead, dull, meaningless, debatable book.

Many steps that we take are debatable and uncertain. I am writing this in an airplane somewhere over Colorado. Whether or not we arrive in Chicago is debatable. Will I arrive at my motel without a car accident, assuming we land safely? It's debatable. Is my bank safe? It's debatable. Is my investment safe? It's debatable.

Any of these things can be debated. Any of them can be doubted.

I don't move on the basis of my doubts. I move on the basis of my faith. I'll soon know if my faith in this airplane was well-founded. (It was.)

You may begin your quest for awakening a love for God and His commandments with many doubts. Accept them and take a step of faith. You will soon discover whether your doubts are well-founded or ill-founded. Let me assure you that your step of faith will be rewarded. But you must begin by even putting faith in God's statement.

CAUTION /

There is a preliminary step that you must take if God's commandments are to live for you:

> But a natural man does not accept the things of the Spirit of God: for they are foolishness to him; and he cannot understand them, because they are spiritually appraised (1 Cor. 2:14).

> He who is of God hears the words of God; for this reason you do not hear them, because you are not of God (John 8:47).

What does that mean? It's like saying that calculus is meaningless to the reader unless he has a mathematical background.

Likewise, the Bible is dead to you unless you have the Spirit of God within you. It is said of Jesus:

> Behold, I stand at the door and knock: if any one hears My voice and opens the door, I will come in to him, and will dine with him, and he with Me (Rev. 3:20).

> But as many as received Him, to them He gave the right to become children of God, even to those who believe in His name (John 1:12).

Granted, these statements are debatable and subject to doubt. As an act of faith, open the door and He will come in and empower you to become a child of God.

Then, and only then, will you discover the truth of the words of Jesus when He said:

> He who has My commandments and keeps them, he it is who loves Me ... and I will love him and will disclose Myself to him (John 14:21).

Then His commandments will come alive and you will discover whether it is indeed true that they will lead you to peace, joy, stability, and blessing.

STEP 2: LOVING YOUR NEIGHBOR /

Jesus said:

> A second is like [the first commandment], "You shall love your neighbor as yourself" (Matt. 22:39).

Now, that's a strange statement. How is keeping His commandments the same as loving people? I don't understand it. Neither do I understand how water can be snow, ice, and steam. Or how electricity can heat, refrigerate, and produce light. I don't need to understand it just to use it. Jesus said:

> This is My commandment, that you love one another, just as I have loved you. Greater love has no one than this, that one lay down his life for his friend (John 15:12-13).

The apostle Paul said:

> For the whole law is fulfilled in one word, in the statement, "You shall love your neighbor as yourself" (Gal. 5:14).

It doesn't take much reflection to realize that loving beats hating. Both of them happen underneath your skin. We are all familiar with the misery of being filled with hatred.

If Jesus commands us to love and Paul says it fulfills all the commandments, shouldn't we take it seriously?

STEP 3: LOVE YOURSELF /

We now move on to step 3. The brevity of my treatment of step 2 doesn't mean that it isn't important. But I have learned that the simplest way to get people started on keeping His commandments is to get them working on themselves:

> You shall love your neighbor *as yourself* (Matt. 22:39).

This is another way of saying that I must have a sense of improvement in my attitude and reactions to all the people who cross my path. I must be pleased with my behavior toward them.

More important, I must have a growing sense of self-respect. I need to like myself. Imagine living day in and day out being repulsed by yourself.

I have spent a lifetime listening to the stories of people who don't like themselves. The details of these stories vary greatly, but gradually I've become aware of recurring themes as I listen to people tell me about themselves—how they chip away at their own self-respect, which leads to personal anxiety and misery, as well as trouble with other people.

FIVE WAYS TO BUILD SELF-RESPECT /

These recurring themes fall into five categories and are usually given in this order:
1. Your behavior
2. Your talk
3. Your reactions
4. Your thoughts
5. Your goals

TAKE INVENTORY /

Behavior. Just think about what you have done this week. Some of your behavior was commendable, sacrificial, far beyond the call of duty. However, some behavior may not have been commendable, but selfish, reluctant, far less than your best.

Words. Think of some of the words you've used—words of praise, of reassurance. There were helpful, constructive, supportive words. Then there might have been some murmuring, complaining, griping, nasty words— even lies.

Reactions. What you do is observable and what

you say can be heard. But the way you react to what's been said and done is not readily observable or audible. This is the invisible, private part of your world.

You may have sensed love, joy, peace, gentleness, tenderness, appreciation within you.

On the other hand, you may have nursed some hatred, bitterness, anger, rebellion, envy.

Thoughts. Another invisible, private part of your world is your mind. No one can observe your thoughts. You can be thinking wholesome, positive, constructive, complimentary thoughts.

On the other hand, your mind can be filled with negative, destructive, uncomplimentary thoughts—even if you look angelic.

Goals. Then, there are your goals, your purposes in life, your objectives. You may have positive, constructive goals, or negative, destructive ones. We all have goals. Sometimes our goal is to not have goals. Or to not reveal them.

YOU NEED AN ACCURATE REFERENCE POINT /

Loving yourself begins with self-respect, a good self-image. And the first step to healthy self-respect is locating yourself in five areas: behavior, speech, reactions, thoughts, and goals.

To locate yourself, you need a reference point—a mirror—something to truly reflect and portray where you are right now.

Two men came out of a mine shaft. One had a dirty face. The other man's face was clean.

The man with the clean face looked at his companion, concluded that his own face was also dirty, and left to wash his face.

The dirty-faced man didn't wash up. After seeing his friend's clean face, he decided there was no need.

They used each other as reference points. Both came up with the wrong information. We need a reference point, a mirror, a guidebook that is consistently accurate.

I've used such a guidebook, and in twenty-five

years of counseling I've never found its principles to be incorrect.

That guidebook is the Bible.

NOT ENOUGH TO LOOK IN THE MIRROR /

It's not enough to stand in front of the mirror and see what's wrong. We need to take calm, corrective action. James 1:23-25 tells us:

> For if any one is a hearer of the word and not a doer, he is like a man who looks at his natural face in a mirror; for once he has looked at himself and gone away, he has immediately forgotten what kind of person he was. But one who looks intently at the perfect law, the law of liberty, and abides by it, not having become a forgetful hearer but an effectual doer, this man shall be blessed in what he does.

How can it be said more clearly? Without action your information is not being used to your advantage. You can decide to start.

NO ONE MAKES A LIFETIME COMMITMENT . . . /

A commitment requires a first decision and then a renewal of that decision whenever necessary.

Can you remember the day you borrowed some money from a bank? You committed yourself to repaying that loan, didn't you?

Yet, each time you had an installment come due, you had to recommit yourself to that promise.

LIKE GOING TO COLLEGE /

Can you remember the day you made the initial decision to go to college?

Good. But if you'd stopped there, you'd never have made it through.

Each time a test came along, you had to renew your original commitment and take the test. You had to make daily decisions to study or not to study. You were reaffirming your initial commitment.

When it came time to do your research papers, you had to reaffirm your commitment. To get through college, you had to renew your commitment probably a dozen times a day.

Or you wouldn't make it.

WANT IT BAD ENOUGH? /

If someone wants to do something bad enough, he'll do it.

I knew a young boy who didn't want to go to church. In fact, he resisted church stubbornly. No matter what his parents or friends would say or do, he was determined not to go to church.

He was ready to face the disapproval and pressure of family and friends to stick with his decision. It was a matter of will. He would not go to church!

Then, I've known teen-agers who were just the opposite. No encouragement from home. For a fact, discouragement. Yet, you couldn't keep them from church.

They would get there for the Sunday morning service and get back for the youth group on Sunday evening and stick around for the evening service.

And every Wednesday night they'd be there for prayer meeting. No encouragement from their relatives . . . their schoolmates. It didn't matter.

They always made it to church.

Anyone committed to turning away from early childhood training will do so, regardless of pressures not to do so.

It has been my observation that people who have rejected their early training can also turn from their present behavior.

I've watched people who are consciously wrong and justify it because of their past, then choose to stop being wrong in spite of the past.

I've observed young people adopt an entirely new pattern of behavior after only one year of college and then turn back to their early behavior just as abruptly as they turned away from it.

You can choose to read pornographic literature or you can choose not to.

Likewise, if you make a commitment to study the Bible and live accordingly, no one can stop you.

But, to remind you once again, a commitment

made today will need to be renewed again and again as other opportunities tempt you to divert your time and effort.

COMMITTED TO WHAT? /

The pivotal point leading to a life of joy, peace, and an abundant life is to love the Lord your God with all your heart, and with all your soul, and with all your mind. Jesus said:

> He who has My commandments and keeps them, he it is who loves Me . . . (John 14:21).

It is within your power to decide to know and keep God's commandments. But you must renew that commitment many times a day. There will be many temptations along the way to draw you from your original commitment. The Bible contains a reassuring promise:

> Therefore let him who thinks he stands take heed lest he fall. No temptation has overtaken you but such as is common to man; and God is faithful, who will not allow you to be tempted beyond what you are able, but with the temptation will provide the way of escape also, that you may be able to endure it (1 Cor. 10:12-13).

The next chapters deal with the basis for loving yourself—for becoming indestructible.

4 / Living With Yourself
(Behavior—Part 1)

4 / Living With Yourself (Behavior—Part 1)

YOUR DAILY TASKS BUILD RESPECT—OR TEAR IT DOWN /

One part of your life that either builds self-respect or tears it down is behavior—the choices you make.

Everyone is involved in a multitude of choices every day. Your self-respect depends on the quality of your performance.

> You do your best.
> You do poorly.

> You do it right.
> You mess it up.

> You do what is required.
> You cheat.

> You follow instructions.
> You disobey.

> You give it all you've got.
> You do it half-heartedly.

> You keep your agreements.
> You go back on your word.

These and more are choices you make day after day, according to the principles that guide you. The Bible gives you a central reference point:

> He who has My commandments and keeps them, he it is who loves Me . . . (John 14:21).

BENEFITS OF KEEPING COMMANDMENTS /

There is more to Jesus' words than meets the eye. We mentioned some of the benefits of keeping the commandments on page 34. This is such a critical choice that I want to elaborate. Consider some statements from wise King David:

KNOWLEDGE OF SIN /

Thy word have I treasured in my heart, that I may not sin against Thee (Ps. 119:11).

INSIGHT AND UNDERSTANDING /

I have more insight than all my teachers, for Thy testimonies are my meditation. I understand more than the aged, because I have observed thy precepts. I have restrained my feet from every evil way, that I may keep Thy word (Ps. 119:99-100).

PEACE AND STABILITY /

Those who love Thy law have great peace, and nothing causes them to stumble (Ps. 119:165).

The prophet Isaiah and the Book of Joshua add more insights:

WELL-BEING AND RIGHTEOUSNESS /

If only you had paid attention to My commandments! Then your well-being would have been like a river, and your righteousness like the waves of the sea (Isa. 48:18).

PROSPEROUS AND SUCCESSFUL /

This book of the law shall not depart from your mouth, but you shall meditate on it day and night, so that you may be careful to do according to all that is written in it; for then you will make your way prosperous, and then you will have success (Josh. 1:8).

Searching out all those commandments will lead you into a lifetime study of the Bible. Also, it will guide you into conduct pleasing to God and will contribute to your own self-respect.

That's worth a lifetime of study, for, why not commit yourself to a lifetime of doing what is right? Just as people who are physically fit spend a lifetime seeking out fitness principles and following them, so contented people learn the principles that will enable them to build self-respect . . . to love themselves.

BROAD BIBLICAL GUIDELINES /

The Bible furnishes us with some broad guidelines to help us make choices, but what it says puts the responsibility for our daily actions squarely on our own shoulders:

> All things are lawful for me, but not all things are profitable . . . I will not be mastered by anything (1 Cor. 6:12).
>
> All things are lawful, but not all things edify (1 Cor. 10:23).
>
> . . . to one who knows the right thing . . . and does not do it . . . it is sin (James 4:17).
>
> The work of righteousness will be peace, and the service of righteousness, quietness and confidence forever (Isa. 32:17).

Every day of your life you make choices about what you will or will not do. In part, the joy of participating in athletics is the challenge of making quick, spontaneous decisions within the rules and boundaries of the game.

Likewise, the pleasure and fascination of life is in making decision upon decision within the commands God gives us.

Continuous, ongoing study of God's commandments with the intent to obey them is a most satisfying life style.

Consider this example of how one man saw his self-respect grow by the choices he made.

WHICH WAY TO TURN? /

Fred came to me with a unique question. He was an expert skier, a member of an Olympic team. He was a very popular athlete—one of the favorites of the sports-writers.

As a result, his picture and favorable write-ups appeared constantly in newspapers across the country. Because of his popularity, a ski manufacturer was urging him to turn professional and to endorse their skis. This meant an income of at least $50,000 annually.

The Olympic committee was urging him to remain an amateur. He was the spark plug of the ski team. Fred was

I WANT HAPPINESS NOW!

torn between his loyalty to the amateur team and the lure of the professional contract.

Finally, Fred agreed to remain an amateur until after the national meet, which would be held in the Rocky Mountains the first week of February.

But the ski manufacturer kept after him, and got him to promise to turn pro after the amateur meet and in time to race in the professional championships the third week of February.

NO SNOW IN THE ROCKIES /

The first week of February there was not enough snow in the Rockies, so the meet was moved to New Hampshire, but because of other meets already scheduled in that area, the date was changed to the third week of February.

What was he to do?

The amateur committee insisted that the change in dates did not release him from his promise. But the ski manufacturer had a promise from him, also. He got conflicting advice from attorneys and friends.

"What does a person do?" he asked. "My reputation means more to me than the money. It has never before failed to snow in the Rockies. What do you do when the weather crosses you up? I want to keep my word to the amateurs and I want to turn professional."

There were no simple answers. We prayed together for wisdom. But, after prayer, the problem remained.

Finally, Fred realized he must take a step of faith. He would stay with the amateur team. His decision involved a great financial loss, but he was at peace with himself because as best he knew, he did what was right.

Thinking about Fred, a Scripture verse comes to mind:

> Let us not lose heart in doing good, for in due time we shall reap if we do not grow weary (Gal. 6:9).

Making "good" choices is not always easy. For Fred, there was no obvious way to go. His choices had to be determined by the broad "commandments" he was committed to follow.

48

DEBATABLE CHOICE? /

Sid was traveling with his father-in-law. During the trip they had a long conversation about what was right and wrong. They stopped for lunch and, before resuming their journey, his father-in-law stopped at a pay phone to make a call. When he hung up, six dimes were returned in the money return slot.

His father-in-law put them back into the phone box.

"What are you doing?" Sid asked. "That's your good fortune if the phone doesn't work right."

"Not for me."

Sid and his father-in-law had a "twenty-five mile" discussion about the six dimes. Sid remained unconvinced that it was wrong to keep the money. Even his father-in-law admitted that his decision was debatable.

The punch line to this story came a few months later. Sid was using a pay phone, and when he hung up the phone released two dimes. He happily put them into his pocket and drove off. But his decision bothered him.

He told himself that he was fortunate, but he kept thinking he was wrong. Finally, he pulled up to another pay phone and inserted the two dimes.

Was he right or wrong? He wasn't sure, but he was relieved. Deciding is often difficult.

For Sid, this was one of those times. But there is a clear principle involved. The intent to do right, the effort to practice righteousness, leads to peace. Your choices are within your own control.

A CLEAR-CUT CHOICE /

On the other hand, many choices are clearly right or wrong. When I was a boy, we lived in the suburbs. A neighbor had a fine raspberry patch. My instructions were to stay out of that patch—unless permission was given by my parents and the people who owned the patch.

One day I wandered past the patch. The berries were ripe, and there was no one around. I slipped into the patch and started eating—cool, juicy raspberries. What a pleasure!

Suddenly, there was a noise behind me. I turned around and was face to face with the owner. Instantly, I was a bundle of tensions. My heart pounded wildly, and I began to sweat.

Desperately, I pleaded with the lady not to tell my mother. But she wouldn't promise. Those delicious berries suddenly felt like a rock in my stomach as I headed away from the scene of the crime. I was even fearful of seeing *them* again. For the rest of the day, a nagging question plagued my mind: had she told my mother? I had a miserable afternoon.

SURELY, SHE KNOWS! /

This was a conscious, deliberate choice to do wrong. Now, I was suffering agony because of it. Soon, I heard my mother call:

"Hennnnnrrrreeee!"

Did she know? Had the neighbor lady called mom? What would happen to me? Filled with fear and tension, I went into the house, expecting the worst. My mother looked up.

"Henry . . ."

"Yes, mom." *Scared to death. Here it comes.*

"Henry, I want you to go to the store."

What a relief! Maybe she didn't know. But how could I tell?

At dinner, I was fidgety and nervous. Finally, my father said:

"What's wrong with you?"

"Nothing wrong with me, dad. Nothing at all. Nothing." I realized I had protested too much. *I'm going to give myself away if I don't calm down.*

"Then, why don't you eat?"

"I'm eating."

I was eating but the food gave me a sick feeling. I glanced nervously back and forth between my father and mother. Finally, she said:

"Henry, there *is too* something wrong with you."

"Nothing wrong, mom." I resisted the temptation to say it again, then got out of there as quickly as possible.

DAYS OF AGONIZED MISERY /

It was a terrible evening. The frightening climax came when dad called. Usually, when he called me, something was up. Again there was the same reaction within me—tension, sweating, and a pounding heart.

"It's bedtime!" That's all he said.

Whew. What a relief to disappear into the bedroom. But, it proved to be a most uncomfortable night.

The next day I was playing outside and, to my dismay, here came the lady who owned the raspberry patch. I ducked behind a corner of the house, and spied on her as she approached.

She came closer. Closer. Closer.

Then, she went past the house. And on down the street.

Whew. Safe again.

So it went for days of agonized misery. And I never did find out if she told my parents.

NERVOUS, ANXIOUS, WORRIED PEOPLE /

I've listened to countless stories in the consulting room of people who create similar tensions for themselves because of their own actions. No one knows their secret. *But they know.*

And that's enough.

Two lines of a poem—I don't know who wrote them—sum up my point:

> There is a secret in his breast
> That will never let him rest.

Your secret may not be that you robbed a bank or murdered someone. It can be as simple as sneaking into a raspberry patch.

TELEGRAM IN THE NIGHT /

Many years ago I was dean of men in a srnall college. One night, I had to deliver a telegram to one of the students in the men's dormitory. Another student was standing in the hall, so I greeted him and went on to deliver the message.

On my way out, the same student approached me and said:

"I need to talk to you. Do you have a few minutes?"

As we strolled down the sidewalk, he blurted out:

"I have a confession to make. Every time I see you coming toward me I think you have found out what I have done. I'm tired of the suspense of hiding, and want to confess."

He had repeatedly broken a rule that required students who had cars to have liability insurance if they transported other students. He had no such insurance. Often, he would load his car with fellow students and take off. They often joked about how easy it was to put one over on the dean.

They were right. I had no idea this was going on.

Can you picture this student? I'd often stop him on the sidewalk and make small talk. Simple pleasantries (I thought).

"How are you?"

"How is your car working?"

"Good-by."

Occasionally, I'd see him sitting on a bench with his girl friend (who often went riding with him), so I'd wander over to visit a few minutes with both of them.

"It's bad enough when you'd stop me on the sidewalk. But when you'd come over toward where we were sitting on a bench, I'd get all tensed up and nervous. We always figured you had found us out, but then you'd just ask a few questions and walk away."

THEN . . . FRAMED IN THE DOORWAY . . . HERE CAME THE DEAN /

This is what the student had lived with. Then, suddenly this evening, the door opened. There, framed in the doorway and coming right at him, was the dean of men. He figured I was after him, but I walked right past without much more than a word.

"It shook me up when you came in," he said. "I just can't stand it any more."

He was the author of his own misery because of his

52

own behavior—chipping away at his own self-respect.

This student is not unusual. Most of the people I talk to have done what they wanted to do if they wanted to do it bad enough—rules or no rules, promises or no promises, standards or no standards.

When we do so, we must live with whatever tension goes with it—sometimes much and sometimes little. You don't break God's laws (disobey authority) without paying a personal price of inner tension.

WHAT TO DO WITH A BURNING CIGAR? /

Some years ago, I taught a college-age Sunday school class. There was one young man in the class who often said:

"I am very devoted to the Lord. Because my body is the Lord's, I want to take care of it. I don't stay up late, I'm careful what I eat, I exercise regularly, don't drink, smoke—or chase women."

We all listened—and nodded. It's good to know that your students take your teaching seriously.

"Good for you," we would say.

Then, one day at an airport many miles from home, as I was approaching the terminal, I thought I saw this model student standing in front of the building.

Guess what?

He had a cigar in his mouth, puffing away as happy as could be. He didn't notice me. Since he was in my Sunday school class, I walked up to chat with him. Then he saw me—and did a very strange thing.

He stuck that cigar—still smoking—in his pocket.

Isn't a pocket a strange place to put a lighted cigar? He wasn't very happy to see me. One would think he would be glad to see his Sunday school teacher, especially this far from home.

Exactly the opposite.

He was in a hurry to be off.

It was a pitiful, yet amusing, sight. As we talked, the smoke began curling up from his pocket. My pupil was one miserable young man.

What was wrong? He was the architect of his own

misery. His conduct didn't fit his words.

A Scripture verse pointedly summarizes the personal benefit of practicing righteousness:

> Thou hast loved righteousness, and hated wickedness; therefore God, Thy God, has anointed Thee with the oil of joy above Thy fellows (Ps. 45:7).

THE FIRST ACT OF CONCEALMENT /

A statement by Phillips Brooks gives a positive basis for happy living:

> To keep clear of concealment, to keep clear of the need of concealment, to do nothing which he might not do out on the middle of Boston Common at noonday—I cannot say how more and more that seems to me to be the glory of a young man's life.
>
> It is an awful hour when the first necessity of hiding something comes. The whole life is different thenceforth. When there are questions to be feared and eyes to be avoided and subjects which must not be touched, then the bloom of life is gone. Put off that day as long as possible. Put it off forever if you can. Can your actions stand publicity?

SPEED TRAP AT 3:00 A.M? /

I recall traveling along a two-lane highway early one morning—about 3 A.M.

The speed limit posted at the entrance of a little town was 20 miles per hour. I had been traveling 60 and was not about to slow down, not at three o'clock in the morning.

And . . . I didn't.

Kawhoom! I barreled through that little town, realizing that if the town marshall was awake, I'd get a ticket.

There didn't seem to be a soul around as I hurtled through that wide spot in the road.

I kept looking in my rear-view mirror, half expecting to see a car lurching from some side street and heading after me—red light flashing.

But there was nothing. Finally, I hit the "Resume Safe Speed" sign. This was it. I had gotten away with breaking the law. I looked back in the mirror, greatly relieved.

It reminds me of the Bible verse already quoted:

> The work of righteousness will be peace, and the service of righteousness, quietness and confidence forever (Isa. 32:17).

WHY IS HE FOLLOWING ME? /

Have you ever been driving on a freeway and suddenly spotted a state trooper cruising behind you?

Why is he following me?

You glance at your speedometer.

I'm only going 55.

Isn't that a comfortable feeling? The relief of correct behavior.

Recently, I was riding in a friend's car. We were in a hurry to get to an office but couldn't find a parking place. So he decided to take a chance on putting the car in a No Parking area.

Rarely have I done business so quickly. My friend was pressing the entire time—and very relieved to get back out on the street!

The student, my friend, and I are all alike. *We do what we want to.*

When we violate our own commitments, we must live with the tension that accompanies it. We don't break God's laws without paying a personal price.

"THAT'S A DUMB SIGN!" /

Recently I was on an elevator. There was a "No Smoking" sign on the wall. A man got on with a lighted cigarette. He said:

"That's a dumb sign."

It may be, but he was violating it. And he knew it.

There are many signs that tell us what to do:

Wait to Be Seated	Visitors Only
No Parking	Quiet Please
Remit Before the 15th	One Way
Keep Off the Grass	Turn Left

There is no end. Many rules to be obeyed. Play within the rules, and you're comfortable. Do otherwise, and you're uncomfortable. Consider what the Bible has to say:

> . . . each one examine his own work . . . in regard to himself

alone, and not in regard to another (Gal. 6:4).

. . . want to have no fear of authority? Do what is good, and you will have praise of the same . . . if you do what is evil, be afraid . . . for . . . an avenger . . . brings wrath upon the one who practices evil (Rom. 13:3-4).

A WORD ABOUT GUILT /

I have found guilt is only a problem with people who pretend to be sorry for something they have done, but intend to do it again.

Guilt is no problem to the repentant person, no matter what he has done, if there is a willingness not to repeat the mistake.

If you follow God's commandments, you will watch your self-respect grow, and you will be on the way to becoming indestructible.

5 / Living With Others
(Behavior—Part 2)

5 / Living With Others (Behavior—Part 2)

WHAT ABOUT THE REST OF THE WORLD? /

You have to live with yourself. But what about the rest of the world? Your behavior toward others is just as important to building self-respect.

Interacting with people often reveals unexpected, self-centered behavior.

AROUND THE WORLD /

One time a mission executive for whom I had worked many years as his consultant invited me to take a tour with him. We were good friends.

Finally, after a year of planning, we met in Switzerland to begin a journey that would take us around the world. Our flight was called. The exit from the terminal to the plane was a door just wide enough for one person at a time to pass through.

Since I was the executive's consultant and wanted to be "cooperative and agreeable," it seemed reasonable to suggest:

"You go first."

"No, you go first," he replied.

"No, *you* go first, I insisted.

Finally, I reluctantly gave in and went through the door first. To get into the airplane we had to climb a narrow stairway. On the way to the stairway I told myself:

So help me, he is going up first. I said to him:

"You go first." He came back with:

"No, you go first."

We were stymied at the foot of that ladder.

Finally, *he gave in* and went up the ladder first. I felt better. We got inside the plane, and there were two seats. Now the question was, Who gets to sit by the window?

I wanted that seat and figured that if I offered it to him first, he would refuse and I could get it. Sure enough that's what happened.

"Why don't you take the window seat?" I said to him.

"No, you take the window seat," he answered. Pretending reluctance I "gave in" and took it.

This gentleman and I were friends. There was respect, admiration, good will between us. We liked each other. He had a Th.D. degree, and I had a Ph.D. degree.

That's a lot going for a relationship, isn't it? How much education and friendship does it take for two men to get along smoothly? We had three problems *before we even sat down on the plane.* Isn't that something?

We looked at each other sheepishly and agreed that we would surely have a hard time getting around the world.

THE INEVITABLE DEADLOCK /

What was the basic problem?

First, both he and I had to face a simple truth. He wanted to run things his own way. I wanted to run things my way. In a word—selfishness. We fit the picture of human nature as described in Isaiah 53:6:

> All of us like sheep have gone astray, Each of us has turned to his own way; but the LORD has caused the iniquity of us all to fall on Him.

Second, he and I, individually, needed to repent of this self-centeredness, to be forgiven, and cleansed—which we did.

Third, if we were to manage the multitude of daily decisions that come up on a tour, we needed a leader to give direction.

WHO WOULD YOU VOTE FOR? /

So, we called ourselves together to have an election. But we faced the thorny problem of choosing a leader with only two people voting.

Which one of us would you pick to be the leader? In order to help you decide, let me give you some facts. He was the director of the mission. His people were expecting him. Most of them had never heard of me.

Now, readers, let me tell you what happens whenever I ask my audiences to choose one of us for a leader on the basis of the above facts. The dialogue between me and the audience goes something like this:

> *Brandt:* Let me ask you folks out there . . . how many of you would vote for me to be the leader?

(Not a single hand goes up.)

> *Brandt:* Let me run through that question again!

(There is hilarious laughter, but no one changes a vote.)

Everyone votes for the mission director. I wouldn't vote for me either. He was the obvious leader.

I still had my Ph.D. My experience didn't disappear. My reputation didn't change. It wasn't a matter of my losing face because he was now the leader. We had simply decided, among friends, which one of us would have the last word. This way we could get to our common goal without a debate every time a little decision was needed.

We had no more problems on our trip, even though my opinion still differed with his at times. He made the final decisions, many times following my judgment. Our respect for one another grew. But we could have been bitter enemies by the time the trip was over.

THE BASICS WORKED /

There are a few basic principles that governed our choices.

First, we were both committed to following the commandments as our guide for living.

Second, we consciously acted on our commitment. Here are two verses that gave us some guidance:

61

Be subject to one another in the fear of Christ (Eph. 5:21).

The fear of the Lord is to hate evil; pride and arrogance and the evil way (Prov. 8:13).

If you put these verses together, they simply mean that two men who "fear Christ" are not two cringing, fearful people, but rather two men who would want to clear away any evil, pride, or arrogance that is revealed between them and figure out a mutually agreeable way to get along.

It's fun to cooperate.

LINDA'S FAMILY /

Linda's family lives in an affluent neighborhood with plush evergreens, hedges, and an enclosed swimming pool.

In some ways, this lushness excites Linda and her mother. In other ways, it galls them, because all is not well in the midst of this luxury.

Linda's dad is an insurance representative in four states and is away from home much of the time. He gives his wife a specified allowance each month, tells her exactly how to spend it, and checks up on her spending regularly.

Linda hears her mother and father argue on a regular basis. The issues are usually the same—his long absences from home, not paying any attention to Linda, and his tight-fisted control over the money.

THE ARGUMENTS ARE ALWAYS THE SAME /

Recently, Linda and her mom were discussing Linda's latest problem.

"Mother, I just have to get some new dresses. Let's face it, kids at this school dress like dreams. I'll never be accepted if I can't keep in step. Just two weeks from tonight, we're having a party, and I haven't a thing. . . ."

"Linda, you know your father insists that I buy you too many clothes as it is."

"LINDA, DON'T CRY!" /

"Isn't there something we can do, mother? I'll just die if the kids won't accept me. I just know I won't be invited to another party unless. . . ."

Linda began sobbing.

Linda's mother usually yielded to her husband's instructions, even if she inwardly resented them.

This time she rebelled and made a decision she knew her husband would object to.

"Linda, don't cry. I'll try to cut down on something else so you can have more new clothes. I hope your father won't notice. So be careful. If he finds out, there will be trouble."

"Oh, I will, mother. Don't worry."

Their plan worked. Before the party, Linda had some new clothes. As she dressed, Linda thought of her father.

Would he notice and question her?

She needn't have worried about that, though. Linda's father was much too preoccupied to notice her clothes.

DAD MAKES AN OBSERVATION /

One night, however, when Linda came home wearing a new dress, her father did remark:

"You look very nice in that dress."

"Thank you, dad," she replied, as she felt herself beginning to blush. Nothing more was said.

SECOND THOUGHTS /

In her room, Linda had some serious misgivings about their scheme. Then, as she remembered the way the kids had been impressed with her new attire, she said to herself:

Oh, well. I guess all's fair in love and war—as long as you don't get caught. It's all dad's fault anyway. If he'd give mom more money she wouldn't have to cheat.

THE PRINCIPAL CALLS /

A month of seeming serenity passed. Then, Linda's mother's world caved in. On a Friday, the school principal phoned, asking about Linda's health.

"I'm so sorry she's had the flu. I've received your note." When the principal stopped talking and hung up,

Linda's mom was numb with disbelief.

Tears filled her eyes. She sat down. She hadn't written any note. Linda hadn't been sick.

Linda had been skipping school. But why? Why would she do such a thing to me? We are so close!

Linda's mother decided to do something about it. She brought Linda to me.

THE CONSULTATION /

Several consultations followed with all the members of the family. There was ill-will, selfishness, and deception in the hearts of all of them.

Linda's father *was* unreasonable. There was plenty of money available. As it turned out, his wife did have plenty of money to spend. The issue turned out to be how to spend it, not how much.

Linda did have many dresses. It was not a question of enough dresses—only more of the same.

What then is the point of the illustration? It is this. Linda's mother was chipping away at her own self-respect by purchasing more dresses and entering into a conspiracy with her daughter to deceive her husband. She had the ground cut out from under her when she learned that her daughter was also deceiving her by skipping school. How could she deal with her daughter's deception when she, herself, was deceiving her husband?

THREE PEOPLE: EACH HURTING HIMSELF /

Linda's mother justified her own choices by telling herself she was being a considerate mother—exactly the opposite of her inconsiderate husband.

He was, indeed, an inconsiderate husband and a disinterested father. His world revolved around himself and his own interests. He did not really need to be away as often as he was. He justified his choices by telling himself that his business demanded the life style he chose for himself.

Linda was becoming a skilled manipulator, doing as she pleased, and she justified her choices by convincing herself that she was only doing what was necessary to be accepted by her friends because she was a neglected child.

I once read a description that applies to all three:

> Bobby is bounded on the north by Bobby, on the south by Bobby, and on the east and west by Bobby.

This family would benefit greatly if they would be guided by some biblical principles like this one:

> Do nothing from selfishness or empty conceit, but with humility of mind let each of you regard one another as more important than himself; Do not merely look out for your own personal interests, but also for the interests of others (Phil. 2:3-4).

I have listened to many similar stories and I have found out that we are capable of an endless variety of ways of deceiving ourselves. The Bible puts it clearly:

> The heart is more deceitful than all else and is desperately sick; who can understand it? I, the Lord, search the heart. I test the mind, even to give each man according to his ways, according to the results of his deeds (Jer. 17:9-10).

Knowing that our hearts are deceitful, and knowing that God will search our hearts and test our minds, it is only logical to continuously submit our choices to the test. But how? The psalmist gives a clue:

> Search me, O God, and know my heart; try me and know my anxious thoughts; and see if there be any hurtful way in me, and lead me in the everlasting way (Ps. 139:23-24).

James says it also:

> But prove yourselves doers of the word, and not merely hearers who delude themselves. For if any one is a hearer of the word and not a doer, he is like a man who looks at his face in a mirror; for once he has looked at himself and gone away, he has immediately forgotten what kind of person he was (James 1:22-24).

You can know your heart, if you allow the Lord to show you yourself reflected in His Word. On the basis of what you see, you can act on His instructions:

> Let the wicked forsake his way, and the unrighteous man his thoughts; and let him return to the Lord, and He will have compassion on him, and to our God, for He will abundantly pardon (Isa. 55:7).

The apostle John points the way to a carefree life:

> Little children, let us not love with word or with tongue, but in deed and in truth. We shall know by this that we are of the truth, and shall assure our heart before Him, in whatever our heart condemns us: for God is greater than our heart, and knows all things. Beloved, if our heart does not condemn us, we have confidence before God; and whatever we ask we receive from Him, because we keep His commandments and do the things that are pleasing in His sight (1 John 3:18-22).

SOME GUIDELINES TO HELP /

The Bible gives some guidelines for making choices:

1. *Treat others as you would like to be treated.* Jesus said:

> And just as you want men to treat you, treat them in the same way (Luke 6:31).

This is the so-called Golden Rule. It requires serious self-study, rather than concentration on figuring out someone else.

How would you like to be treated?

Would you like others to make an effort to find out what pleases you?

Would you like others (when they find out what pleases you) to defer to your wishes rather than theirs when there is a difference of opinion?

Do you mind being deceived or lied to?

Would you rather serve or be served?

Do you mind if people say one thing to you and another when you aren't there?

According to the Golden Rule, we are to treat others as we would like to be treated rather than try to second-guess the other person. Come to think of it, that's good news for the other person.

2. *Be a leader.* The apostle Paul says:

> The things which you have learned and received and heard and seen in me, practice these things; and the God of peace shall be with you (Phil. 4:9).

A first reading of this verse gives us the impression

that it is a hopelessly egotistical and impossible statement. On second thought, what a wonderful goal! Imagine, living your life in such a fashion that anyone who pays close attention to you finds the God of peace is with them because they follow what they learn, receive, hear, and see from you. They, like you, are making choices that are commendable, positive, and wholesome. Such a description of yourself is surely a firm foundation for building your self-respect, your self-love.

3. *Make choices as though the Lord were beside you—thankfully.* The apostle Paul says:

> And whatever you do in word or deed, do all in the name of the Lord Jesus, giving thanks through Him to God the Father (Col. 3:17).

A moment's reflection, and you realize the presence of your boss, a policeman, or even a stranger in your home is enough reason to pay careful attention to your behavior. Imagine how careful you would be if the Lord were with you.

Such choices—within the limits of His commandments—would surely result in a thankful spirit. You would be thankful because your choices are building your own self-respect.

4. *Carry out your choices heartily, and desire to please God.*

> Whatever you do, do your work heartily, as for the Lord rather than for men; knowing that from the Lord you will receive the reward of the inheritance. It is the Lord Christ whom you serve (Col. 3:23-24).

There is nothing more frustrating than doing things reluctantly, unwillingly. Boredom is one of our nation's greatest plagues.

Sooner or later, everyone is faced with tasks to do that you would rather not do. There are chores, housekeeping, errands, duties at work or at church—to name a few.

Has it ever occurred to you how many nostrils and throats a physician examines in a day? Or how many mouths a dentist peers into in a day? There is no need to pity these people. If they have a healthy response to their work, they accept the routine along with the glory.

All of us have no choice about many of the duties we must perform. Everyone can ask God for a hearty spirit toward the task if he wants to.

How wonderful to enjoy what you are doing—to do it heartily—to do it as an act of worship! This is true whether your work is at the desk, at the bench, in the shop, behind a podium, in the home. The poet has aptly put this thought into words:

> Let me but do my work from day to day,
>   In field or forest, at desk or loom,
>   In roaring market-place or tranquil room;
> Let me but find it in my heart to say,
> When vagrant wishes beckon me astray,
>   "This is my work; my blessing, not my doom;
>   Of all who live, I am the one by whom
>   This work can best be done in the right way."
>
> Then shall I see it not too great, nor small,
>   To suit my spirit and to prove my powers;
>   Then shall I cheerful greet the laboring hours,
> And cheerful turn, when the long shadows fall
> At eventide, to play and love and rest,
> Because I know for me my work is best.
>
> Henry Van Dyke

A twentieth-century prophet, A. W. Tozer, has expressed the same principle:

> We must offer all of our acts to God and believe that He accepts them, then hold firmly to that position, and keep insisting that every act of every hour of every day and night be included. . . . Let us practice the fine art of making every work a priestly ministration. Let us believe that God is in all of our simple deeds and learn to find Him there.
>
> Whatever ye do, do your work heartily, as for the Lord rather than for men; knowing that from the Lord you will receive the reward of the inheritance. It is the Lord Christ whom you serve (Col. 3:23-24).

Clearly then, to perform all our deeds to bring honor to His name, to please Him, and to do it in the spirit of thankfulness and heartiness is to build our self-respect, our self-love.

IF YOU DON'T . . . /

One important reason for this is that behavior

which falls short of biblical standards will cause you unrest, anxiety, worry, and tension. You pay a great price when you depart from truth, integrity, and honesty.

A goal for you might be the same one that Paul gave to Timothy:

> Let no one look down on your youthfulness, but rather in speech, conduct, love, faith and purity, show yourself an example of those who believe (1 Tim. 4:12).

> Be imitators of me, just as I also am of Christ (1 Cor. 11:1).

CONCLUSION /

Everyone, every day, faces a multitude of choices. Your sense of self-respect, of loving yourself, depends upon making those choices within the framework of commandments you choose to follow.

Consider seriously what Jesus told His disciples:

> Teaching them to observe all that I commanded you; and, lo, I am with you always, even to the end of the age (Matt. 28:20).

Finally, consider these verses:

> All Scripture is inspired by God and profitable for teaching, for reproof, for correction, for training in righteousness; that the man of God may be adequate, equipped for every good work (2 Tim. 3:16-17).

If you use God's commandments as the basis for your behavior, you are on the way to becoming indestructible.

6 / Evaluating the Way You Talk

6 / Evaluating the Way You Talk

WORDS, WORDS, WORDS . . . /

The use of words is the most common subject that comes up in my consulting room. This is a difficult subject to write about, because words get tangled up with the emotions as well as with a person's mental activity.

With words, we compliment and praise one another. Our words can be comforting, helpful, supportive, instructive, revealing all those good things that are on our minds.

. . . I'M SO SICK OF WORDS /

On the other hand, words can cut, hurt, tear someone up without leaving a mark. Words can be used to deceive, mislead, or conceal what is on your mind.

> They speak falsehood to one another; with flattering lips . . . they speak (Ps. 12:2).
>
> The tongue is a deadly arrow; it speaks deceit; with his mouth one speaks peace to his neighbor, but inwardly he sets an ambush for him (Jer. 9:8).
>
> Do you see a man who is hasty in his words? There is more hope for a fool than for him (Prov. 29:20).

Many people have long ago forgotten the spankings received as a child but can recall vividly some of the tongue lashings and hostile criticisms received along the way.

Married couples who seek counsel have long ago forgotten the tender words exchanged among themselves but can easily recall some of the stinging, sarcastic, critical, deceptive words that seem to weld themselves on their minds. As the Bible puts it:

> For we all stumble in many ways. If any one does not stumble in what he says, he is a perfect man, able to bridle the whole body as well. Now if we put the bits into the horses' mouths so that they may obey us, we direct their entire body as well. Behold, the ships also, though they are so great and are driven by strong winds, are still directed by a very small rudder, wherever the inclination of the pilot desires. So also the tongue is a small part of the body, and yet it boasts of great things. Behold, how great a forest is set aflame by such a small fire! And the tongue is a fire, the very world of iniquity; the tongue is set among our members as that which defiles the entire body, and sets on fire the course of our life, and is set on fire by hell. For every species of beasts and birds, of reptiles and creatures of the sea, is tamed, and has been tamed by the human race. But no one can tame the tongue; it is a restless evil and full of deadly poison. With it we bless our Lord and Father; and with it we curse men, who have been made in the likeness of God; from the same mouth come both blessing and cursing. My brethren, these things ought not to be this way (James 3:2-10).

It is clear that you either build up or chip away at your self-respect by your choice of words.

LOOK AT THE NEGATIVE SIDE /

Hasty, careless, impulsive words can turn a pleasant day into a nightmare.

Wally bounced out of bed in a good mood. He greeted his wife with a friendly hug and kiss. They had a pleasant breakfast together, and after a tender good-by kiss, he headed for the garage—whistling a tune to himself.

He was pleased with himself because he got an early start and would be able to get some desk work out of the way before the start of a busy day.

Everything changed when he put the car key in the switch and glanced at the gas gauge. It was on empty.

"I told that #$%¢&* wife of mine to put gas in the car when she used it last night. And she didn't do it!"

Wally was seething as he waited at the gas pump for the tank to be filled. Already, he was rehearsing what he would say to his wife that night.

It was a busy day, so the gas-tank episode was forgotten until he headed home. The closer he got to home the angrier he became.

Wally slammed the door of his car and headed for the house. He brushed past his wife, mumbling a gruff:

"Hello."

"What's wrong with you?" she asked.

"Nothing!"

"There must be something wrong," she mused.

She pressed for an answer.

"Did you have a rough day at work?" She had no idea what was going on underneath his skin, or she might have had some second thoughts about pursuing the question.

Then he unloaded.

"Yes, I had a rough day. I left early to get some desk work done, only to find an empty gas tank. So instead of getting a head start, I spent my time sitting beside a gas pump.

"Didn't I tell you to put gas in the car? Why don't you listen to me? Why is that I can never depend on you? I'm fed up with your lack of consideration. All you think about is yourself."

His wife burst into tears.

"Quit your bawling," he went on. "Do I have to put up with an emotional woman on top of your irresponsible behavior?"

Before he was halfway through, Wally was sorry he had started his tirade. But once he got started, he figured he might as well finish it.

If his employees ever tried talking to him that way, he would have fired them. He wouldn't think of speaking to his friends the way he just addressed his wife.

By now, the children were listening, too.

"You kids . . . get out of here!" He shoved one of them backward and kept on yelling.

By spewing out this torrent of words, Wally made a fool of himself and felt foolish about it. But the words were out.

He was especially disturbed over his choice of

words and the manner in which he delivered them. This wasn't the first time this happened. He ruined many an evening with his sharp tongue and then had to figure out how to patch things up.

A NASTY TONGUE /

The telephone rang. It was for Ange, the sixteen-year-old daughter in the family.

On the other end of the line was a young man the family didn't approve of—asking Ange to go to a party at the home of another friend Ange's parents didn't approve of. Ange accepted the invitation, hoping to talk her folks into letting her go.

When she hung up, Ange took a stab at changing her parents' minds.

"Can't I please go?" she pleaded.

"You know the answer," her mother replied.

"Aw, come on, please let me go. All the kids but me will be there. Please let me go. Dad, tell mom to let me go."

"You heard your mother. You knew what we would say when you agreed to go."

"Oh, please . . . just this once?"

"The answer is no!" her dad repeated.

Then Ange launched out on a speech.

"You never let me do anything. I hate this place, and I hate you. When I get a little older, you will be sorry, because I'm going to clear out of here and do whatever I please. All you do is make life miserable for me. You must hate me to treat me like you do. None of my friends have to take the guff I take around here. You don't care about me at all. I hate you."

Wow! Quite a tirade for a teen-ager. Her parents kept quiet and let her continue until she ran out of words. She was feeling miserable before she finished.

Actually, Ange didn't disagree with her parents' judgment. But, again and again, she would sass her mother, or tell off the whole family, or lash out at anyone who crossed her. She caused herself no end of trouble socially, and often ended up disgusted with herself.

WHAT'S BEHIND IT ALL? /

These people violated some basic command-ments. Here are some of them:

> He who guards his mouth and his tongue, guards his soul from troubles (Prov. 21:23).
>
> And I say to you, that every careless word that men shall speak, they shall render account for it in the day of judgment. For by your words you shall be justified, and by your words you shall be condemned (Matt. 12:36-37).
>
> He who gives an answer before he hears, it is folly and shame to him (Prov. 18:13).
>
> If any one thinks himself to be religious, and yet does not bridle his tongue but deceives his own heart, this man's religion is worthless (James 1:26).

GRIPING AND COMPLAINING (ROAST BOSS FOR LUNCH) /

Three men who worked together shared a common distaste for their jobs. Every day at the lunch table, they would rehash the rude comments their boss fired at them and discuss with one another how much they despised him.

Their boss was indeed a very difficult man to live with. I suppose everyone sooner or later faces the problem of what to do with a difficult person in life. The Bible says:

> Do all things without grumbling or disputing (Phil. 2:14).
>
> A perverse man spreads strife, and a slanderer separates intimate friends (Prov. 16:28).
>
> . . . malign no one, to be uncontentious, gentle, showing every consideration for all men (Titus 3:2).

These men were chipping away at their own self-respect by their choice of a subject at the lunch table.

LYING AND DECEIVING (ADVICE FROM A GOLF EXPERT) /

Gordy was golfing with Al, who was a par player. On the way to the course, Gordy explained that he was just an occasional golfer and not very good. Al offered to give Gordy some tips as they went along. The offer was accepted.

At first, Gordy appreciated the help.

Watch your head . . . now . . . you need a little

more grass on that shot . . . raise your left shoulder . . . keep your eye on the ball . . . you should use a different club.

On and on went the instructions, until Gordy was getting knots in his stomach. All he really wanted was to knock the ball around the course.

"Want another tip?" Al asked.

Instead of admitting that he was already confused and annoyed, Gordy replied:

"Sure I do. It's not often I get to play with someone who can help my game. You are a good teacher."

His deception and flattery needlessly put him in a position that spoiled his whole day.

LYING TO THE DIRECTOR /

The work director of a college had summoned a student to tell him of a job opening. Before sending him to this assignment, however, the director wanted to clear up a report that this student had been disorderly on various occasions.

The student denied the report and was given the assignment. A week later, he returned to admit that the report was true.

He had been in torment for a week. Even if it meant losing the work opportunity, he wanted to get the record straight.

DECEIVING HIS FRIENDS /

Steve created an unnecessary situation for himself. He was visiting some friends who in turn took him to visit some of their friends. It came time for supper.

"We can go out to eat if you like," said the hostess. "We have every kind of restaurant you can think of around here. Or, since I've made some vegetable soup today, we can stay home and eat that. It makes no difference to me which we do. Since Steve is our guest, and we don't know what he has eaten today, let's let him decide."

That's a tough spot for a guest. Steve answered with a question:

"Does anyone have anything against staying here and eating soup?" All four people said they'd just as soon stay home.

"Great," said Steve. "Then let's just stay here and eat soup."

On the way home from the visit, Steve said to his friends:

"Boy, can I get something to eat? I didn't have any lunch today, and if you noticed, I didn't eat much. I hate soup—especially vegetable soup."

His friends were astounded.

"Why, Steve, we asked you if you wanted something else. Do you think we didn't mean it?"

"Well, I didn't want to offend or inconvenience anyone," Steve said. Instead of gaining admiration for his "sacrificial" choice, his friends wondered when they could believe Steve.

DECEPTION LED TO TENSION /

Mrs. Merton was referred to me by her physician because a reasonable prescription for "nerves" was not helping.

She finally admitted to me that she had lent her car to a friend, who was involved in an accident with the car.

Knowing that her husband would be furious because she had loaned out the car, Mrs. Merton decided to tell him she had been in the accident.

To deceive her husband was simple enough, but she hadn't anticipated the complications: coaching her friend on what to say, keeping her husband away from the collision shop, and slipping police reports past him.

It became especially complicated when the repairs were made poorly and required two extra visits to the garage, which involved the insurance agent over and over again. The cover-up resulted in unbearable and unnecessary tensions for Mrs. Merton.

I frequently listen to people explain their reasons for lying on the grounds that if they were to speak the truth, the other person would hate them, get angry, or have hurt feelings.

What a delusion to assume that the key to good fellowship is lying and deceit. On the other side of the coin, my clients tell me how disappointed they are when they discover they have been deceived or lied to.

Sir Walter Scott penned two pithy lines that caught my attention:

> Oh, what a tangled web we weave,
> When first we practice to deceive!

It is easy to understand why such seemingly insignificant incidents are so disturbing to people when they are aware of what the Bible has to say about lying and deception:

> Lying lips are an abomination to the LORD, but those who deal faithfully are His delight (Prov. 12:22).

> Put away from you a deceitful mouth, and put devious lips far from you (Prov. 4:24).

> There are six things which the LORD hates, yes, seven which are an abomination to Him: haughty eyes, a lying tongue, and hands that shed innocent blood, a heart that devises wicked plans, feet that run rapidly to evil, a false witness who utters lies, and one who spreads strife among brothers (Prov. 6:16-19).

> A lying tongue hates those it crushes, and a flattering mouth works ruin (Prov. 26:28).

GOSSIP AND WHISPERING (THE DAY I "LEFT MY WIFE"!) /

The Bible says:

> The tongue is a small part of the body, and yet it boasts of great things. Behold, how great a forest is set aflame by such a small fire (James 3:5).

A simple little incident that happened to me has made that verse very meaningful. I was once speaking to a large gathering. During one of the breaks, a conferee came up to greet me.

"Hi, Henry, haven't seen you in a long time. Is Eva (my wife) with you?"

"No," I replied. "I left her. . . ." At that moment someone else interrupted by asking a question. I never finished my sentence concerning my wife.

Later that day, a friend's wife approached me and said:

"What's this I hear about you and Eva? You're

separated?"

"Separated?" I was astonished. "Where did you hear that?"

"One of the ladies told me. She heard that you told one of the men that you'd left Eva."

"No, we're getting along just fine," I replied.

"That's strange," she said. "I've heard it from several women."

THIS IS WHAT HAPPENED /

It took me a while to think over my conversations of the day. Then I recalled my brief encounter with the man who asked if Eva was with me.

This is what happened. When I said, "I left Eva . . ." and turned to respond to someone else, he concluded that I didn't want to talk about it. He was troubled and disappointed that I would be speaking about family life when I was separated from my wife.

When he went to his hotel room, his wife was there. So he said to her:

"Did you know that Henry has left Eva?"

His wife asked someone else about it, and so the rumor got started.

Here are the facts. Eva and I were invited to go cruising on a friend's yacht. We were having a grand time enjoying the beauty and peacefulness of the Bahamas.

It came time for me to go to this conference, but it is a long, hard journey from Miami to San Francisco, where the meeting was held.

Our friends urged Eva to stay in the Bahamas with them. I would have liked to stay myself, but we agreed that Eva would stay.

This man wanted to know if Eva was with me. My reply was interrupted by someone else, so all he heard was: "I left her . . ." I never got to finish my sentence: ". . . on a yacht in the Bahamas."

TAKING ON A RUMOR /

The next time I took the platform to speak, I told the entire assembly about the incident as an example of how communications can get fouled up.

Apparently, some people didn't believe me. A year later, in Portland, a minister very gingerly brought up the subject:

"Did you leave your wife?"

THREE YEARS LATER . . . /

Three years later, an associate of mine reported this incident to me. One of his secretaries asked him:

"How can you be associated with Dr. Brandt when he and his wife are separated?"

Behold, how great a forest is set aflame by such a small fire!

AN EDUCATOR IS CHARGED! /

The dean of a college was called into a board meeting to answer charges that at night he was seen prowling around the windows of a women's dormitory.

He was told that there were a dozen witnesses who reported his behavior. It wasn't just one incident. They reported he was seen there regularly.

The dean was flabbergasted. He insisted that there was no truth to the reports. But how could a dozen eyewitnesses be wrong?

Then it dawned on him. The garage that housed the school cars was located behind the women's dormitory. This dean frequently went out at night to speak at various meetings. He used a school car for transportation.

When the board investigated, they found out that his facts were true. One night, after he put the car in the garage, a student was looking out her window and saw the dean walking behind the dormitory.

She was amazed and told her roommate that she saw the dean window peeping.

They told some other students, who, in turn, kept an eye on the back of the dorm to see if it happened again. Sure enough, they spotted him behind the dormitory week after week.

The news spread rapidly throughout the campus and in letters back home to parents: our dean is a window peeper.

GREAT EVILS . . . /

We tend to be aghast when we learn that someone has stolen something or committed adultery, but we little realize how great a fire such a small member as the tongue can set by whispering and gossiping.

"DON'T TELL" INFORMATION /

One day Margaret listened to some "don't tell" information about Sandra, her best friend. The informer was supposed to be one of Sandra's closest friends, too. A few days later, Sandra asked Margaret point-blank:

"Did you hear that I stepped out on my boyfriend last Saturday night?"

Not in the habit of lying, Margaret was forced by the truth to answer: "Yes."

Sandra was stunned.

"Who told you, Margaret? It's important that I know."

Caught between two loyalties, Margaret wished she had not listened to this whispering. Now, it seemed that no matter what she said or didn't say, Margaret stood to lose a friend. That's the danger of secret, don't-say-I-told-you conversations. They lead to strife, tension, and severed relations.

Note what Solomon wrote:

> The words of a whisperer are like dainty morsels, and they go down into the innermost parts of the body (Prov. 18:8).

> For lack of wood the fire goes out, and where there is no whisperer, contention quiets down (Prov. 26:20).

> Accordingly, whatever you have said in the dark shall be heard in the light, and what you have whispered in the inner rooms shall be proclaimed upon the housetops (Luke 12:3).

The Bible says that hasty words, a fiery tongue, concealing your true thoughts, complaining, slandering, lying, deceit, whispering are unacceptable to God.

Your own sense of self-respect depends in part on your knowledge of how you manage your own words.

THE POSTIIVE SIDE /

We described the negative side. There is also a

positive aspect to the use of words. Take a look at these Bible verses:

> A man has joy in an apt answer, and how delightful is a timely word (Prov. 15:23).
>
> Words from the mouth of a wise man are gracious, while the lips of a fool consume him; the beginning of his talking is folly, and the end of it is wicked madness (Eccl. 10:12-13).
>
> Like apples of gold in settings of silver is a word spoken in right circumstances (Prov. 25:11).
>
> Righteous lips are the delight of kings, and he who speaks right is loved (Prov. 16:13).
>
> Pleasant words are a honeycomb, sweet to the soul and healing to the bones (Prov. 16:24).
>
> A gentle answer turns away wrath, but a harsh word stirs up anger (Prov. 15:1).
>
> The tongue of the righteous is as choice silver, the heart of the wicked is worth little (Prov. 10:20).
>
> A soothing tongue is a tree of life, but perversion in it crushes the spirit (Prov. 15:4).

GOOD WORDS IN BAD TIMES /

The Bible story of Joseph gives us a good example. His brothers, who despised him and determined to get rid of him, sold him into slavery.

Joseph, however, after many trials and difficulties, achieved a place in Egypt second only to the king. When a time of famine came, Joseph was given charge of distributing food. His brothers had to go to Egypt to get some food, and were aghast when they discovered who Joseph was.

To compound their fear, their father died during this time. They decided to send Joseph a message, begging for mercy. This was the message:

> "Your father charged before he died, saying, 'Thus you shall say to Joseph, "Please forgive, I beg you, the transgression of your brothers and their sin, for they did you wrong."' And now, please forgive the transgressions of the servants of the God of your father." And Joseph wept when they spoke to him. Then his brothers also came and fell down before him and said: "Behold, we are your servants." But Joseph said to them: "Do not be afraid, for am I in God's place? And as for you, you meant evil against me, but God meant it for good in

order to bring about this present result, to preserve many people alive. So, therefore, do not be afraid; I will provide for you and your little ones." So he comforted them and spoke kindly to them (Gen. 50:16-21).

Comforting, kindly words—backed by appropriate action, and based on Joseph's faith in God, *not on the behavior of his brothers*. What a relief this must have been to them!

USING YOUR TALK TO PUT PEOPLE AT EASE /

A small child accidently spilled her milk. She looked anxiously up at her mother, who quietly said:

"You put your glass too close to your elbow, didn't you?" One could see the relief on the child's face. It certainly was better than just lashing out at the child, wasn't it?

Her words taught the child how to avoid repetition of the incident.

Later that evening, the small child was reluctant to go to bed. Quietly, but firmly, the mother said:

"You are to go to bed!" The child still didn't go, so mother took her by the arm and firmly directed her toward the bedroom.

One could see the child stiffen, and then give up as mother continued:

"You need a good night's sleep."

This mother set the tone in her family by her soft answers that issued from a kind heart, again backed by appropriate action.

Once I told this story to a group of mothers. One lady in the audience was in the habit of giving her children tongue lashings over spilled milk. On the spot, she breathed a prayer of repentance and asked God to teach her to speak lovingly and quietly.

That same night, her child spilled some orange juice. To her surprise, the lady said quietly:

"Next time, keep the glass away from your elbow."

Amazed and wide-eyed, the child looked at her mother and said:

"Would it work if I spilled some milk?"

This lady couldn't wait to tell me about the change

in her the next time our paths crossed. Is it not obvious that such conversation is necessary if we are to have congenial relations with each other?

SOFT TALK IS NOT NECESSARILY "SISSY TALK" OR "WEAK TALK" /

The positive use of words does not imply a namby-pamby spineless person who has no opinions or takes no action. We are surrounded by responsibility for employees, fellow laborers, family members, and friends. Frequently, everyone must deal with the evil intentions of other people.

God said of Himself:

> Those whom I love, I reprove and discipline; be zealous, therefore, and repent (Rev. 3:19).

Jesus, when instructing His disciples, taught them:

> Be on your guard! If your brother sins, rebuke him . . . and if he sins against you seven times a day, and returns to you seven times, saying, "I repent," forgive him (Luke 17:3-4).

In his second letter to Timothy, Paul instructed him:

> Preach the word: be ready in season, and out of season; reprove, rebuke, exhort, with great patience and instruction (2 Tim. 4:2).

Again, Paul instructed Timothy:

> Do not sharply rebuke an older man, but rather appeal to him as a father, to the younger men as brothers, the older women as mothers, and the younger women as sisters, in all purity (1 Tim. 5:1).

To the Ephesians, he wrote:

> Let no unwholesome word proceed from your mouth, but only such a word as is good for edification according to the need of the moment, that it may give grace to those who hear (Eph. 4:29).

A few years ago, I was pondering the meaning of a verse having to do with our relations to one another:

> Let us consider how to stimulate one another to love and good deeds (Heb. 10:24).

While I was mulling over the meaning of that verse, a friend shared the following incident that confirms that passage:

ANGER OVER THE CAR REPAIR /

My friend was involved in a conversation with a man who was very angry over the poor service he was subjected to while getting his car repaired.

As he listened, the thought occurred to him that he should stimulate the angry man to love that mechanic. Surely he would be better off if he could get rid of that anger.

But, how do you proceed without a chance to think it over first?

A statement made by Jesus occurred to my friend, so he decided to give it a try.

"It's a pity to let a mechanic spoil your day. He isn't even here, yet his poor performance is bothering you. Your attitude surely isn't affecting him any. He's on the other side of town. Listen to a statement that Jesus made":

> (God) . . . causes His sun to rise on the evil and the good, and sends rain on the righteous and unrighteous (Matt. 5:45).

"Sure, you got a bad deal. Why don't you just forgive him, and ask God to give you love for him? It would change your whole day."

SURPRISE! /

The man surprised my friend by saying:

"You're right. I'll do it. How stupid of me to allow this to spoil my day."

Instead of an angry response, the man appreciated the tip.

A HELPFUL SUGGESTION /

This incident occurred at a banquet. I was the speaker, seated beside the pastor. It was a family-style banquet, so everyone helped himself. I noted the huge quantity of food he had heaped on his plate. It amazed me to see him take a second helping as large as the first.

He noticed I was aware of what he was doing, and leaned over toward me and said:

"I'm a compulsive eater."

In my mind, I was wondering how to make a stimulating, helpful reply, so I gave it a try.

"There is a better word for it," I said, "and the word is gluttony."

Well, my words did stimulate him. They shocked him.

A year later, I was invited to speak in the same church at the same banquet. What a surprise! The pastor was slimmed down, and was not a bit overweight.

His wife told me that my words indeed challenged him. He even looked up the word "gluttony" in the Greek. He decided that his eating habits were a stumbling block to his people and were not pleasing to God.

But he surprised me by saying:

"You are heavier than you were a year ago."

EATING MY OWN WORDS /

"Yes," I explained, "speaking at so many banquets, luncheons, and breakfasts makes it difficult to watch what you eat."

"There is a better word for it," he replied gleefully. "It's called gluttony."

He gave my little speech right back into my teeth. We have become good friends. We stimulate each other. It's a good relationship. Whenever I head toward his part of the country, I am reminded of how we helped each other.

To stimulate, reprove, rebuke, exhort, instruct one another is to help one another. It's a personally rewarding experience to purpose in your heart to be a postive influence with your words. In writing to Timothy, Paul says:

> Retain the standard of sound words which you have heard from me, in the faith and love which are in Christ Jesus (2 Tim. 1:13).

TALK . . . POSITIVE! /

The positive side of using words as indicated in the Bible involves pleasant, righteous, soothing, gentle, kindly words: a soft answer, wholesome, stimulating, reproving, rebuking, exhorting words; with simplicity and godly sincerity.

So, along with David the psalmist, a good objective for anyone can be as he stated it:

> Let the words of my mouth, and the meditation of my heart be acceptable in Thy sight, O LORD, my rock and my redeemer (Ps. 19:14).

> Set a guard, O LORD, over my mouth; keep watch over the door of my lips (Ps. 141:3).

> Who is the man who desires life, and loves length of days that he may see good? Keep your tongue from evil . . . and do good, seek peace, and pursue it (Ps. 34:12-14).

SOME TIPS FOR RESTORING FELLOWSHIP /

1. When you are aware that someone has something against you, it's your move. Jesus says:

> If therefore you are presenting your offering at the altar, and there remember that you brother has something against you, leave your offering there before the altar, and go your way; first be reconciled to your brother, and then come and present your offering (Matt. 5:23-24).

2. When you have something against someone else, it's your move. Jesus says again:

> If your brother sins, go and reprove him in private; if he listens to you, you have won your brother. But if he does not listen to you, take one or two more with you, so that by the mouth of two or three witnesses every fact may be confirmed. And if he refuses to listen to them, tell it to the church; and if he refuses to listen even to the church, let him be to you as a Gentile and a tax-gatherer (Matt. 18:15-17).

What is Jesus saying? Simply that whether you have something against someone, or someone has something against you . . . *either way it's your move to go to that person* and go out of your way to attempt a reconciliation.

CAUTION /

It is not enough to attempt reconciliation if you go with a hostile spirit. The apostle Paul adds another touch:

> But speaking the truth in love, we are to grow up in all aspects into Him who is the head, even Christ (Eph. 4:15).

The goal, then, is not only reconciliation, but also helping each other grow up. You build your own self-respect or self-love as you speak *to* people rather than *about* them.

A REMINDER /

Even if you accept the goals for your words as described in this chapter, be reminded of the problem facing you:

> Their tongue is a deadly arrow; it speaks deceit; with his mouth one speaks peace to his neighbor, but inwardly he sets an ambush for him. Shall I not punish them for these things? (Jer. 9:8).

Your only hope is to turn to God for help. What he will do for you is described by Isaiah the prophet:

> The Lord GOD has given me the tongue of disciples, that I may know how to sustain the weary one with a word. He awakens Me morning by morning, he awakens My ear to listen as a disciple (Isa. 50:4).

If you use the Bible as your guide for your choice of words, you are on the road to building up your self-respect and becoming indestructible.

7 / Your Inner Life: Feelings and Emotions

7 / Your Inner Life: Feelings and Emotions

TWO COUPLES /

It's remarkable how differently people respond to the same set of circumstances. A supervisor of volunteer summer workers shared an experience that illustrates what I mean.

He placed two couples on an island populated with disadvantaged people. Each couple was to take a specified area and establish a recreational program for the children and a Bible-study program for the adults. When the supervisor visited the island two weeks later to see how the work was progressing, he found the first couple disgusted, sullen, depressed.

"We hate this place," they said.

"The children are wild, unmanageable. They swear and have lice in their hair. The adults are unfriendly. They come to our meetings an hour late or not at all. Most of them sleep through the meeting.

"We hate the taste of the water and can't stand living in this dump. We want out."

Then the supervisor visited the second couple. When they opened the door, he was greeted warmly by two people whose faces were covered with soot.

"Come on in," they said.

"Our oil stove just exploded. A few minutes ago everything was clean, and then: 'BANG!'

"Look at this mess. Come on, help us clean it up."

As they worked on the cleanup job, this couple went on to describe their experience.

"We found out that when we tried to teach these people about love and responsibility and cleanliness, they didn't know what we were talking about. The kids are wild, and the adults won't cooperate, so we got mad at them. We stayed away from them for a few days and just tried to justify our own nasty attitudes.

"Then, it dawned on us that we weren't loving and responsible either—just clean. We recalled our studies about Jesus:

> He came to His own, and those who were His own did not receive Him (John 1:11).

> But God demonstrates His own love toward us, in that while we were yet sinners, Christ died for us (Rom. 5:8).

"We thanked God for showing us what we were like, and asked Him to forgive us and give us a loving, responsible spirit. He did, and what a change. Now, we love it here. What a challenge." Then, the husband said:

"Hey, do you want to go fishing? A week ago, I spotted some men getting into a boat, so I jumped in, too, and asked to go along. They didn't like it, but before the day was over, they quit ignoring me. Now, they even invite me to go along and have taught me how to filet the fish, and have showed me where the fishing holes are. I think my new attitude made the difference.

"The kids still don't want our program, and the adults ignore our Bible studies, but we keep at it and we love it."

Two couples—living in the same place with the same people. What sharply contrasting reactions.

THE MOST IMPORTANT SUBJECT—REACTIONS /

Reactions involve *your inner life.*

The management of your inner life is, to me, the most important subject in this book.

Every day you will either reveal or conceal feelings, emotions, attitudes, intentions and thoughts stimulated by people and events. Either way, whether you reveal or conceal them, there they are, coming from within you.

You can't control what other people do around

you. Neither can you control all the events of the day. How you respond will either build up or chip away at your self-respect and self-love, depending on how you manage what goes on underneath your skin.

PLEASANT, POSITIVE FEELINGS AND EMOTIONS /

When psychologists write about the inner life, they refer to pleasant and unpleasant feelings, or positive and negative emotions. There are two kinds of pleasant feelings and emotions.

First, when there is a highly pleasurable and satisfying response to people or circumstances, we describe ourselves as excited, elated, thrilled, ecstatic, exhilarated.

Recently I heard a TV advertisement inviting people to experience a "new high" at a certain resort. Along with such pleasant responses come some bodily changes like a pounding heart, increase in respiration rate, muscle tension. Such responses are easily experienced at an athletic contest, a suspense drama, a concert, when anticipating some event, on the arrival of a special friend or relative, in the presence of someone, or while participating in something challenging.

It takes a lot of energy to sustain such a condition and there comes a point when this excitement, pleasant as it is, must cease, or it becomes unpleasant.

Second, a person can be described as living heartily, joyously, happily when the inner life is described as calm, still, quiet.

Muscles are relaxed, heartbeat is normal, digestion is normal. There is freedom from nervousness. All these words describe an inner condition that can be summed up in one word: *peace.*

Feeling good and pleasant *today* is not a sure test of whether the feelings are built on a firm foundation. One can be filled with elation, pleasure, and joy over successfully cheating, stealing, lying, deceiving, sensuality, breaking the law, going through a divorce, expressing cruelty and selfishness.

In the long run, good feelings not based squarely on God's commandments will turn to ashes.

UNPLEASANT, NEGATIVE FEELINGS AND EMOTIONS /

The person who experiences unpleasant feelings and negative emotions can be described as being filled with tension, restlessness, anxiety, frustration. He probably has tense muscles, a pounding heart, faulty digestion and nervousness.

These words describe an inner condition also, and can be summed up in one word: *misery*.

The pace of modern-day living is crisis upon crisis—rapid, unpredictable change in people and circumstances.

A common response to the pace is misery: tension that invades the soul and even the nervous system.

We can't endure misery. Something must be done about it. Peace must be restored.

There is general agreement among physicians, psychiatrists, psychologists, and ministers regarding the destructive effect of the so-called unpleasant feelings and negative emotions that result from the absence of peace.

OUT OF CONTROL EMOTIONALLY? SO'S YOUR BODY /

O. Spurgeon English, then chairman of the Department of Psychiatry at the Temple University Medical School, wrote once of a long study of the relationship between mind, the emotions, and the body.

He said there are certain emotional centers in the brain linked to the entire body through the autonomic nervous system. He described charges of emotions that are relayed from the brain, down the spinal cord and through the autonomic nerves to the blood vessels, muscle tissues, mucous membranes, and skin.

Under emotional stress, he points out, all parts of the body can be subject to physical discomfort because of a change in blood nourishment, glandular function, or muscle tone.

You may have asked, "How can thoughts and feelings going through my mind cause pain in some part of my body far from my brain?" Dr. English explains: An emotion such as fear, he says, can cause the mouth to become dry. This means that the blood vessels have constricted and the blood supply and glandular activity have been reduced. This dryness will occur, for example, in someone who must make a speech and is afraid.

Laboratory tests show that under stress of emotion the same decrease in glandular activity occurs in the mucous membrane and various parts of the digestive tract.

Not only does the blood supply change markedly, but secretions of various types increase or decrease in an abnormal manner. Changes in muscle tone in the digestive region can occur, causing painful cramps.

It has also been proved that emotional stress will increase the size of the blood vessels in the head, and this can produce pain because of the stretching of the tissues around the blood vessels and their pressure on the nerve endings.

Of the heart, Dr. English says:

"Without the presence of any heart disease whatever, psychosomatic patients are prone to increased heart rate, irregularities of rhythm, unusual sensation about the heart such as oppression, tightening, pain, and numbness sometimes accompanied by shortness of breath and the feeling of faintness and weakness, possibly giddiness. Along with this so-called 'spell' there may be a general 'all-gone' feeling, free perspiration, accompanied by a sinking sensation and the feeling as if the patient would fall in a heap.

THE BODY PICKS UP UNSOLVED PROBLEMS /

"For decades," he says, "it has been known that a personality problem which cannot be solved by the mind itself is prone to be 'turned over' or 'taken up' by some other part of the body.

"When an irritating friend or a troublesome family member cannot be coped with, the patient becomes 'sick,' he can't 'stomach' it or it 'gripes' him. The physician knows that the cause of these gastrointestinal disturbances is emotional conflict. He knows it is the attitudes of generosity and responsibility struggling with an opposing wish to escape them."

Dr. English then lists the emotions involved. Here

they are:

Hatred, resentment, rage, frustration, ambition, self-centeredness, envy, jealousy, sorrow, love need, fear.

These are the emotions that describe reactions to someone or something that gets in your way. They are unpleasant and cause disturbing bodily changes.

"WORN, TIRED . . . ALMOST HELPLESS" /

Two psychologists, Strecker and Appel, describe the relationship of emotions and bodily changes:

"If aroused to a high pitch, shame, distress, hate, envy, jealousy all strike to the very core of our being. They leave us worn, tired, incapable, and almost helpless.

"The blush of shame, the haggard countenance of distress, the consuming burning of jealousy and envy, and the facial and vocal expressions of hate are striking testimonials to the deteriorating effect of these emotions upon the body. We may jump with joy or droop with sorrow."

THE EFFECTS OF HATRED /

S. I. McMillen, a physican skillful in writing as well as in practicing medicine, speaks of the devastating effect of hatred:

"The moment I start hating a man, I become his slave. I can't enjoy my work any more because he even controls my thoughts. My resentments produce too many stress hormones in my body, and I become fatigued after only a few hours or work. The work I formerly enjoyed is now drudgery.

"Even vacations cease to give me pleasure. It may be a luxurious car that I drive along a lake fringed with the autumnal beauty of maple, oak, and birch. As far as my experience of pleasure is concerned, I might as well be driving a wagon in mud and rain.

"The man I hate hounds me wherever I go. I can't escape his tyrannical grasp on my mind. When the waiter serves me porterhouse steak with French fries, asparagus, crisp salad, and strawberry shortcake, smothered with ice cream, it might as well be stale bread and water. My teeth chew the food and I swallow it, but the man I hate will not permit me to enjoy it. . . .

"The man I hate may be many miles from my bedroom; but more cruel than any slave driver, he whips my thoughts into such a frenzy that my innerspring mattress becomes a rack of torture. The lowliest of the serfs can sleep, but not I. I really must acknowledge the fact that I am a slave to every man on whom I pour the vials of my wrath."

EMOTIONS THAT DESTROY US /

The emotions that cause tension, anxiety, and frustration, as noted by the four authors—a psychiatrist, two psychologists, and a physician—are:

hatred	self-centeredness
resentment	ambition
rage	envy
frustration	jealousy
love need	sorrow
shame	fear

Their presence, whether expressed or held in, lead to misery, tension. No one needs to learn how to respond this way. It comes as naturally as breathing. Such responses begin at birth, as anyone can testify who has tried to quiet a baby or a small child.

Take a look at some Bible verses that describe the same responses as violations of God's commandments and therefore, when they exist within, this condition chips away at your self-respect and self-love.

You will note that modern-day research has only confirmed what this ancient book has described centuries ago:

GOD'S VIEWPOINT /

Cease from anger, and forsake wrath; Fret not yourself, it leads only to evil doing (Ps. 37:8-9).

Do not be eager in your heart to be angry, for anger resides in the bosom of fools (Eccl. 7:9).

I am benumbed and badly crushed; I groan because of the agitation of my heart (Ps. 38:8).

Better is a dish of vegetables where love is, than a fatted ox and hatred with it (Prov. 15:17).

A tranquil heart is life to the body, but passion is rottenness to the bones (Prov. 14:30).

Fret not yourself because of evildoers, Be not envious toward wrongdoers (Ps. 37:1).

Let us not become boastful, challenging one another, envying one another (Gal. 5:26).

The wicked flee when no one is pursuing, but the righteous are bold as a lion (Prov. 28:1).

For where jealousy and selfish ambition exist, there is disorder and every evil thing (James 3:16).

Even the simple details of life will stimulate such reactions if they are within us. Why must we find a way to eliminate them? Because they are intolerable, too unpleasant to live with, and the bodily changes that go along with them are too painful and uncomfortable to ignore. We are forced to find relief, peace, quiet.

Let me share a few incidents as described by my clients:

HOW ANGER, HATE, AND BITTERNESS RUINED A VACATION /

Alton and Joan, his wife, went on a skiing vacation. It was to be a pleasant, relaxing time. No problems. They arrived, checked in at their motel, and were even able to change their reservation from a more expensive room to a cheaper room, which pleased them. They had a pleasant week with evenings spent around the fireplace after a day of skiing.

Finally, it was over. Reluctantly, they went down to check out—only to run head on into an unexpected complication: they had to pay the more expensive rate for their room. They argued, but the management stood firm:

"You reserved a room at the expensive rate, so we're charging you that rate whether you stayed in that room or not."

Alton bitterly paid the more expensive rate and went muttering to the car. As they drove away, he fumed and fussed.

Their entire week was ruined. Suddenly, they couldn't find one thing positive about the whole week in

100

spite of the fact it had been a perfect week until checkout time.

That glorious week of skiing was clouded by what was really a dirty trick.

What had really ruined their week?

The decision of the management?

No. It was the couple's reactions to that decision. They were filled with hateful, angry, bitter emotions that wiped out a beautiful experience.

THE EMPTINESS OF POPULARITY /

Joe came to see me because his marriage had collapsed. He was depressed, disillusioned, and a flop as a salesman.

It wasn't like this a few years back. Joe, from a small town, enrolled in a major university and went out for football. He hardly expected to make the team. Then the regular fullback broke his ankle, and Joe was picked at random to run some plays. To everyone's surprise, he became the starter.

What followed were three years of weekly headlines, interviews, the roar of the crowd, and autograph seekers. He was allowed to choose easy courses, and his teachers gave him good grades for very little work.

Joe loved every minute of it. He was completely and happily taken up with the attention and popularity that was his, and his choice of pretty girls on and off campus.

NEXT . . . THE WORLD /

After graduation, at age twenty-three, Joe was sobered to realize he was unprepared for any kind of work. His reputation got him into an executive training program, but he quickly dropped out for lack of basic knowledge.

All he knew was football. When he was stripped of the glamor of being a varsity football player, all he had left was a big body going soft. He was no longer sought after, and his big body became a liability.

Without any knowledge or skills, and a badly mismatched marriage, Joe suddenly had to face the fact that he had been on a glamorous, pleasant, sensuous road that led to a dead end.

Now, his life was empty. Three happy years of incredible popularity turned to ashes, and he was miserable, bitter, frustrated.

THE FRUSTRATIONS OF DEALING WITH REBELLIOUS BEHAVIOR /

Mr. Somers provided his family with a beautiful, roomy home and plenty of money. But the children drove him wild.

For instance, one evening, while the family was having a delicious meal, one of the children refused to eat the peas on his plate. Mr. Somers was determined that the child eat them.

The child flatly refused, so his father threatened a spanking.

"STOP PUSHING HIM!" /

Mr. Somers' wife told him to stop pushing. Angrily, he continued the issue, finally slapping the child. Mrs. Somers started a heated argument with him.

Finally, he stormed out of the room, and they ended up not speaking to each other for a week.

We would think that two college graduates could resolve such a simple issue. Mr. Somers had no problem with his wife or the child when they did what he asked. Nor did she have any problem when she got her own way.

They both agreed that hostility and stubbornness over so simple a matter was an inappropriate response, and it turned their lovely home into a battleground.

THREE SIMPLE CONFLICTS /

Kelley was enraged because he couldn't take two glasses of orange juice instead of one as he went through a cafeteria line.

His wife was furious when their preschooler spilled her milk.

Pete became highly agitated when two people pressed in ahead of him in a ticket line. On the way home, he was angry because the traffic moved slowly.

Strange, isn't it, that simple, normal details of life

can stimulate emotions that are as intense as if we were facing a major crisis.

What can be done about it?

TWO KINDS OF PEACE /

When speaking to His disciples, Jesus once said:

> Peace I leave with you; My peace I give to you; not as the world gives . . . (John 14:27).

He says there are two kinds of peace:
1. The kind Jesus gives.
2. The kind this world gives.
We will examine both.

THIS WORLD'S PEACE /

Jesus said that in this world we can find peace, but He made it clear that it's not His peace. In this world we can find release from tension in mind and body.

EXERCISE /

Golf courses, tennis courts, paddle, racquet, and handball courts, swimming pools, running tracks, bicycle and hiking paths, various kinds of health clubs, water skiing, snow skiing, bowling alleys are available everywhere.

Anyone who lives heartily, joyously, and happily, who is calm, still, and quiet should have have some kind of exercise program to keep the body in shape.

This is clearly not the same as a person who has an exercise program in order to work off tensions, restlessness, and anxiety—or one who exercises to find relief from mental, emotional, and bodily stresses and strains.

MUSCLE RELAXATION /

There are many study courses offered by high schools, colleges, and professionals that teach us how to relax our muscles from head to toe.

Recently, I watched a television program that featured a Hindu swami giving a relaxation demonstration. He sat for fifteen minutes without moving a muscle while an announcer described the philosophy behind what the swami was doing.

Many years ago, I worked for a maternal health

foundation. We had a division that pioneered in the field of teaching pregnant women how to relax during pregnancy and childbirth. The program worked wonders. This is now common practice all over the country.

Multiplied thousands of women are grateful for such help which gives them a more comfortable, less painful pregnancy.

QUIET ACTIVITY /

There is an endless supply of books available on every conceivable subject. We can lose ourselves by watching television, listening to the radio or records.

There are hundreds of table games available and an endless variety of hobbies, many college and professional athletic teams to watch, many varieties of entertainment.

BUSINESS /

There is a kind of elation, joy, fascination, and pleasure that comes from working, promotions, making money, success, praise, use of a skill, meeting people, entertaining, romance, travel, civic or church work, and getting an education.

CHANGE /

We can remove ourselves from certain people, change jobs, change fields, move to another location, or run away from an unacceptable task.

There is private therapy and group therapy available that enables us to explore the mind and emotions. We can change our philosophy, our standards, and morals.

Multitudes today seek peace by kicking over the traces, living it up, asserting their independence, doing their own thing, discovering themselves.

CHEMICALS /

We are a pill-popping society. We can buy uppers and downers . . . or a chemical to put us to sleep. Thousands use the hard drugs. A major source for calming us down is the use of alcohol. Long ago, Shakespeare said:

> Oh God! That men should put an enemy in their mouths to
> steal away their brains.

What a fascinating list of ways to deal with today's tension. Yes, it's a great world, with endless ways to find peace.

WE DON'T NEED TO TRY EVERYTHING /

King Solomon, who is described in the Bible as the wisest and richest of men, wrote of his efforts to taste of everything life has to offer. He sampled wisdom, mirth and pleasure, wine and folly; he built houses, vineyards, orchards, gardens.

He had servants and maidens, silver and gold. The Book of Ecclesiastes contains twelve chapters describing his quest. He concluded:

> Thus I considered all my activities which my hands had done
> and the labor which I had exerted, and behold all was vanity
> and striving after wind and there was no profit under the sun
> (Eccl. 2:11).

Sooner or later, all our efforts to find peace from this world turn to ashes. When we slow down or are trapped by circumstances and people, the tension, restlessness, anxiety, and frustration return.

The activities available to us can help relieve the effects of unpleasant feelings and negative emotions, but can't remove them. Multitudes of retired people will testify to that.

GOD'S KIND OF PEACE /

There is a deeper kind of peace than the kind that simply relieves body and mind. It comes when you yield yourself to God and let His peace invade your soul. At various times, Jesus said:

> Come to Me, all who are weary and heavy laden, and I will
> give you rest. Take My yoke upon you, and learn from Me,
> for I am gentle and humble in heart; and you shall find rest for
> your souls (Matt. 11:28-29).

> These things I have spoken to you, that My joy may be in you,
> and that your joy may be made full (John 15:11).

These things I have spoken to you, that in Me you may have peace. In the world you have tribulation, but take courage; I have overcome the world (John 16:33).

The apostle Paul, too, points us to God's peace.

Now may the God of hope fill you with all joy and peace in believing, that you may abound in hope by the power of the Holy Spirit (Rom. 15:13).

Be anxious for nothing, but in everything by prayer and supplication with thanksgiving let your requests be made known to God. And the peace of God, which surpasses all comprehension, shall guard your hearts and your minds in Christ Jesus (Phil. 4:6-7).

Strengthened with all power, according to His glorious might, for the attaining of all steadfastness and patience; joyously (Col. 1:11).

King David, also one of the wisest of all men, learned of God's advice to . . .

Cease striving and know that I am God (Ps. 46:10).

HOW TO TAP GOD'S PEACE /

How do you approach God? Jesus said about Himself:

I am the way, and the truth and the life; no one comes to the Father, but through Me (John 14:6).

Behold, I stand at the door and knock; if any one hears My voice and opens the door, I will come in to him, and will dine with him, and he with Me (Rev. 3:20).

There was a man named Nicodemus, a ruler of the Jews. You can read an account of him in John 3.

This man came to Jesus one night and said to Him:

"Rabbi, we know that You have come from God as a teacher; for no one can do these signs that You do unless God is with him." Jesus answered and said to him: "Truly, truly I say to you, unless one is born again, he cannot see the kingdom of God . . ." (John 3:2-3).

"For God so loved the world, that He gave His only begotten son, that whoever believes in Him should not perish, but have eternal life" (John 3:16).

We stumble over the simplicity of this simple step. You are born again—or saved—when you believe Jesus. He said that you have access to the peace of God through Him.

The starting point is when you ask Him to invade your life . . . when you open the door and invite Him in.

He said: "I will come in." You either can or can't point to a moment in your life when you made that decision.

Yesterday, I proposed this step to a disturbed client. He became more disturbed.

"Don't hand me that stuff," he said. "I've asked God for help many times, and it doesn't work."

"When did you ask Him to come into your life?" I asked.

"I've been a Christian all my life," he said. "I grew up in church."

I persisted. "When did you ask Him to come into your life?"

"I can't remember," he said.

To make this step more clear to Him, I asked if he remembered when he purchased his last car.

That he could remember. He also admitted, when I asked, that he purchased the car by a specific action. He didn't purchase it by simply thinking about it . . . or about its construction . . . or by considering all the standard equipment, etc. Only when he agreed to the deal did he purchase the car. He definitely remembered that.

He also remembered exactly when he got married, when he accepted airplane tickets for his last flight, when he accepted his present job.

You are born again when you ask Jesus to invade your life. Otherwise, it's no deal. Jesus is the way to God's peace.

To let Him into your life gives you access to the resources of God: peace, joy, hope, patience.

Then you can put everything and everyone into His hands. You need not be in a dither over anything. You can stop striving and let His peace guard your heart, mind, and body.

It does not follow that because you have access to strength from God that you will give Him your troubles, injustices, hates, hostility, conflicts, ill will. You can, but you can also nurse them within your body.

Let me share with you a struggle that I went through even though Jesus was in my life.

MY BOSS . . . THE SELF-MADE MAN /

An unavoidable confrontation with my own reactions occurred during World War II. I was an engineer in a department responsible for designing some of the tools necessary for the production of vital airplane engines. We were under great pressure to get our work done. There was a good deal of bickering and jealousy between us.

My boss was a mean, tobacco-chewing, self-made man who had worked himself up from the production line to chief engineer.

THE SPITTOON /

There was a large window in the wall of his office facing our department, so we could see each other. Inside his office was an odd arrangement. Beside his desk was a piece of rubber matting three feet in diameter.

In the center of the mat sat a highly polished brass spittoon.

Frequently, we engineers would spot the boss loading his jaw with tobacco. When he finished, his jaw looked like he had an apple in his cheek. When he started to chew, we all braced ourselves because we knew someone was in trouble.

"BRRRAAAANNNNNNNNNNDDDDDDDDTTTTTT!" /

Then, he would spit in the general direction of the spittoon (he seldom hit it) and shout someone's name with all the ferocity of an Indian war cry:

"Brandt! Brraaaannnnnnddddddttt!"

I instantly became furious. One word from him and I was fighting mad. I hated him, and his messy, ugly spittoon.

Of course, you don't tell the boss off. I developed the art of entering his office with a friendly smile on my face and talking to him in a cordial manner, all the time hatefully seething within and contemplating his chin.

AN ACT YOU CAN'T PLAY FOREVER /

No man can keep up an act like that twenty-four hours every day, so I would take out my frustration on my wife and child at home.

"Turn down that radio!" I screamed at my wife.

"Get out of my way." Or: "Pick up that toy, now," I'd yell at our three-year-old. If he didn't jump when I thought he should, I'd swat him all out of proportion to what he'd done.

I'd always be ashamed of myself and determine over and over again not to talk and act (really . . . it was reacting) like that. But it kept happening.

There were some very tense evenings created by my spirit and my tongue. I dreaded going home because of the scene I might create there.

My conduct around my boss and family is clearly described in the Bible:

> His speech was smoother than butter, but his heart was war; his words were softer than oil, yet there were drawn swords (Ps. 55:21).
>
> Even in laughter the heart may be in pain, and the end of joy may be grief (Prov. 14:13).
>
> A quick-tempered man acts foolishly, and a man of evil devices is hated (Prov. 14:17).

At the time, I had no knowledge of the Bible, so these verses were unknown to me.

With my stomach in knots and under constant tension, I had to do something. My choice was to seek a solution out of the Bible. My search led me to some disturbing verses. For example:

> Be angry, and yet do not sin; do not let the sun go down on your anger (Eph. 4:26).
>
> Let all bitterness and wrath and anger, and clamor, and slander be put away from you along with all malice (Eph. 4:31).

What's wrong with being angry and bitter and malicious toward my boss? I argued with myself.

And, how can I turn off my anger at sundown? Besides, if he didn't yell, and if my wife were more under-

standing, and if our child would behave, I wouldn't be angry in the first place.

These verses struck me as unrealistic, unreasonable, and the source of more tension. But another verse was even more disturbing:

> And be kind to one another, tender-hearted, forgiving each other, just as God in Christ also has forgiven you (Eph. 4:32).

I had no intention of responding that way toward my boss, or toward my wife when she was indifferent to my problems. After all, I felt I was entitled to nurse my grudges.

But my misery continued. I finally concluded that when my body was filled with tensions and hostility and my mind was loaded with ugly thoughts, my inner condition surely wasn't affecting my boss, my wife, or my child. They didn't live underneath my skin.

The Bible was right. To be kind, tender-hearted, and forgiving made sense. I would crank up my will power and determination and push the hate, anger, bitterness, and self-pity out of my body. What a relief that would be.

GOOD INTENTIONS GONE BAD /

A few days later, however, came a bitter disappointment. The boss had finished loading his jaw with tobacco and was getting ready to spit.

Somehow, I just knew my name would follow the spit and found myself tensing up. When he yelled ''Brrraaannnddttt,'' I was as furious as ever.

This was disappointing and frustrating to me. I was trying to live up to what the Bible said and couldn't do it. And I was still a growling tyrant around the house.

I went through a period of time being bitter toward God and sputtering about the Bible. *Here was a book that described a way of behaving that couldn't be lived up to.*

But I continued my search, and one day came upon some verses that gave me the answer and changed my whole inner life:

> And such confidence we have through Christ toward God. Not that we are adequate in ourselves to consider anything as coming from ourselves, but our adequacy is from God (2 Cor. 3:4-5).

That verse stopped me. It just wasn't true. I was not inadequate. I had gotten an education without God's help. I got a job, some promotions, made some good investments, engaged in sports, lived up to the etiquette book, controlled myself without God's help.

I mention this because I see many people who isolate Bible verses and reject them or are guided by them without considering the verses that precede or follow the one in question. Instead of reading on, they react negatively as I did.

After a few days of rejecting that verse, I read the next one—which contains a life-changing key:

> Who also made us adequate as servants of a new covenant, not of the letter, but of the Spirit; for the letter kills, but the Spirit gives life (2 Cor. 3:6).

Consider that thought. Anyone can obey the letter of the law. *It's a man's spirit that he can't control.* I could do whatever my boss asked, while at the same time rebel inwardly.

It was the rebellion I couldn't eliminate. I could speak with him in a cordial manner. It was my hostility, anger, and hatred that I couldn't eliminate. I could even control my temper at home if I tried hard enough. It was the temper itself I couldn't eliminate. Even my three-year-old child could make me angry. I could refrain from whomping him, but I couldn't eliminate the anger.

Living up to the letter of what was required of me was killing me. That's where the inadequacy was. That truth was like a shaft of light.

I asked God to help me love my boss, my wife, and child—to keep my body quiet when things didn't go right. A few days later my boss was again loading his jaw with tobacco. He aimed some at the spittoon and let out his war whoop:

"Brrrraaaaaaaannnnnnnnnddddddddttttttt!"

I heard it, but I was quiet. This was unbelievable.

I wasn't angry.

My inner life matched my manner for the first time. What a relief! His antics began to amuse me. I had a new spirit whenever I would let God give me quietness—at work, at home, anywhere. This simple relationship with God changed my life and even my profession. God would quiet my spirit whenever I let Him. Gradually, I have learned to lean on God's peace more and more.

I've spent the last thirty-five years helping thousands of people find peace in the inner man by tapping into the Spirit of God who gives us quietness that can't be interrupted by people or circumstances.

IT WORKS FOR OTHERS, TOO /

I was telling this story to a group of people recently at a conference. The next day, a lady told me her story.

She had had continuous headaches for several years. Medical tests and x-rays could not isolate the cause. Medication didn't help. After listening to my story, she went to her room and told God how she hated the snake of a husband she had divorced several years ago.

She realized she was only punishing herself nursing hatred toward someone who was 3,000 miles away. She asked Jesus to come into her life and give her His Spirit and take the hate away.

She said:

"This is the first day in several years that I didn't have a headache." Four days later, she was still free from her headache.

About a year ago, another lady approached me about her husband. They had been married some twenty years. They were active in religious circles. He was even an elder in the church. But he kept a bottle of vodka in his office and was usually tipsy when he came home. He demanded a hot meal every night, even though his arrival time was unpredictable. Then he expected her to sit with him to watch television and pour his drinks for him.

SHE HAD ENOUGH /

Since the children were out of the house, this relationship had become unbearable. She had never complained to her husband, she said, and faithfully served him. But, she was consumed with rebellion and resentment and anger. She couldn't stand it much longer!

I pointed out to her that she had two problems. Her husband was obviously one of them. He was inconsiderate, selfish, and demanding. But her most serious problem was what went on underneath her skin.

"But I have served him faithfully," she protested. It did appear that her behavior was beyond criticism. She doggedly was living up to the letter of the law. But, God's Spirit was missing.

"But, my husband just thinks about himself."

I listen to this line of reasoning constantly. "My inner life is caused by people or circumstances. How else do you expect me to respond? Am I supposed to enjoy such treatment? Haven't I put up with this long enough? Don't I deserve some consideration, too?"

This dear lady was convinced that her inner life was in the hands of her husband. Several months later, I received a letter from her. It is printed here (in part):

> Nothing has changed in our marriage, but I am contented. I felt so angry with you for what you said to me about myself—but you were right!
>
> Before that I hadn't really recognized my own sin. God had to do some throwing down in my life, and that is never easy at the time, but the result is beautiful if you are submissive to the strong hand of God.
>
> He has forgiven and cleansed and filled my heart with joy. I praise Him for this mercy and grace. Once again, I want to say "thank you" from the depths of my heart.

This letter comes from a lovely young lady who had a breakdown, and when I saw her, she was a nervous wreck. Parts of her letter tell the story:

> I told you my problem was not being invited to join the Junior League, and I really had a hangup about this.
>
> I'd never been interested enough to do all the work and buttering up to League members that it took to get in, so I didn't make it. I was extremely disappointed. I've never felt as crushed or deeply hurt over anything. Most of my friends are member of this group, and I felt completely rejected. I felt guilty that I let my family down and especially my daughter.
>
> I cried and cried over this for hours at a time. So many people could have helped me, and I got mad at them. You helped me to see that I even had the audacity to get mad at Almighty God. Even though I have a Christian husband, a lovely family, and most every material thing I want, I was

miserable. I had told God to just take my life.

I kept telling you my problem was getting left out of the League, and you kept telling me my problem was my attitude toward what happened.

During my second session with you, I asked God to give me his perfect peace. I can't tell you exactly how it happened. The situation remained the same, but God erased all the hurt feelings from me.

I literally felt as if a huge weight had been lifted. Then, I wondered if the peace would last. He brought to my mind that part of John 14, where he says: "My peace I give unto you. Not as the world gives give I unto you."

I'd always thought this verse was just for funerals! Only a couple of times in these three years have I felt a little pang of the old hurt, but each time I immediately thanked God for the peace He'd given me and claimed it.

God even changed my "wants" so that I honestly can't imagine how I ever desired this. Hope this doesn't sound pious.

Another letter tells the same story:

Several years ago, I came to see your for help with my resentment over my husband's insistence on my working in his store when I wanted to spend my time in church work.

You dealt with me about my wretched attitude and I didn't like it. But, I thought it over and came home determined that my work in the store would be a labor of love.

Of course, you know that God filled me with His peace and joy as I worked in the store and worked at being a better wife. It surely is true that our joy is dependent on our relationship with Christ rather than our circumstances or other people—isn't it?

My husband changed his mind about a year ago and agreed that I should get involved in ladies home Bible studies. It's a fine ministry. I thank the Lord that you were honest enough to tell me my faults.

NORMAN LOOKED LIKE A WILD MAN /

When Norman first came to see me he looked like a wild man, with sharp, piercing eyes. The muscles in his face were all tightened up; he drummed his fingers on the table, and jerked his knee constantly. He was a hard, unyielding man. No one crossed him without getting a blast of his vicious temper. His big, strong, heavy-set body made him look dangerous indeed.

But underneath all that was a soul that longed for

peace and a quiet heart. Oh, he argued with me for many months, but today—four years later—this man has quieted down, has a compassionate spirit, and has become increasingly considerate of others. He let God come into his life and clean out that nastiness and replace it with quietness.

THE BRILLIANT ENGINEER /

Ellery is a brilliant engineer. But he didn't come to see me because he had a sprawling home nestled in 200 acres of rolling hills, a jet plane, and a prosperous manufacturing plant that produced more money than he knew what to do with.

He came because he was tired of being an "old crab." His explosive temper made life miserable for his family and employees.

Golf, tennis, good food, travel, and elite surroundings didn't help. He needed to be born again and then allow Jesus to give him His peace.

He couldn't buy it. He had to reach out an empty hand and receive salvation like everyone else. He struggled a long time over this simple proposition, clinging to his insistence that business pressures were his problem, and he was searching for a way to manage himself.

He finally gave up, and reached out that empty hand to receive from God the gift freely given through Jesus.

WHAT ARE THEY SAYING? /

There is a common thread winding through all these stories. In each case, the person involved had (1) done something unacceptable to someone else, (2) someone else had done something unacceptable to them, (3) the person was required to do something he or she didn't want to do, (4) things didn't turn out the way the person wanted them to.

The reactions in each case were similar: anger, bitterness, stubbornness, rebellion, and hate which became intolerable.

In each case, the idea that the people and circumstances involved merely revealed rather than caused their reactions was firmly rejected. The possibility of becoming a loving, peaceful, joyful person without the people or circumstances changing was an unpalatable option. If nothing changed, they preferred to be mad rather that glad.

Isn't it strange that it's so hard to let Christ come into our lives and then let Him change us? We tend to resist Him like a tiny baby will resist its mother's efforts to give it life-providing food.

Strecker and Appel describe this struggle as they observe it in their clients: "Countless people at every corner unnecessarily deprive themselves not only of pleasure, but actual necessities in order to assuage the goading of a troubled conscience and fulfill a need for punishment. Feelings of unworthiness, or undeservedness, result at every hand in conspicuous neglect of health, comfort, and peace of mind.

"The man who, unprovoked, insults his best friend, the man who fails to show up at an important business conference, the girl who refuses an invitation to a party she would very much like to go to, the man who declines to propose to the girl he loves and remains unmarried, the woman who spends endless hours in unnecessary housekeeping drudgery, who 'works her fingers to the bone,' the brilliant man who insists upon engaging in a petty, monotonous routine, a drab, colorless existence, people who seem to court accidents and have always a tale of hard luck, those who repeatedly make plans which seem inevitably to lead to failure—all may be motivated by guilt, the need for punishment or self-directed anger. Added to this are countless hours of sleepless worry, or self-recrimination, self-accusation, bitter regret, which also may be traced to the same source."

Why do we do this to ourselves? Jesus, who knows all about us, says:

> And this is the judgment, that the light is come into the world, and men loved the darkness rather than the light; for their deeds were evil. For everyone who does evil hates the light, and does not come to the light, lest his deeds should be exposed. But he who practices the truth comes to the light, that his deeds may be manifested as having been wrought in God (John 3:19-21).

The prophet Jeremiah gives us another glimpse of the human heart:

> The heart is more deceitful than all else and is desperately sick; who can understand it? I, the LORD, search the heart, I test the mind, even to give to each man according to his ways . . . (Jer. 17:9-10).

There it is. We are at least vaguely aware of our evil inner life, but we hate to admit it. We tend to turn away from such light. The more brilliant and educated we are, the more we are capable of coming up with endless varieties of ways to justify ourselves.

THERE IS A WAY /

Enough of this gloom. There is a brighter side. There is hope. When we finally quit running, the Lord will search our hearts, show us our evil ways, clean us up, and fill us with His strength.

Like any other agreement, this step is taken at a point in time never to be forgotten or confused with other times. But such a crisis works itself out from a point to a line.

It involves a continual drawing upon His resources as each occasion for it comes, just as a decision to maintain an exercise program must be renewed day by day.

In conclusion, take a look at the riches available to you in the inner man—which will build your self-respect . . . your self-love.

THE POSITIVE SIDE /

> Be kind to one another, tender-hearted, forgiving each other, just as God in Christ also has forgiven you (Eph. 4:32).

> And so, as those who have been chosen of God, holy and beloved, put on a heart of compassion, kindness, humility, gentleness and patience; bearing with one another, and forgiving each other, whoever has a complaint against any one; just as the Lord forgave you, so also should you (Col. 3:12-13).

> Let the peace of Christ rule in your hearts, to which indeed you were called in one body, and be thankful (Col. 3:15).

> In everything give thanks; for this is God's will for you in Jesus Christ (1 Thess. 5:18).

> But the wisdom from above is first pure, then peaceable, gentle, reasonable, full of mercy and good fruits, unwavering, without hypocrisy (James 3:17).

> What credit is there if, when you sin and are harshly treated,

you endure it with patience? But, if when you do what is right and suffer for it you patiently endure it, this finds favor with God (1 Peter 2:20).

Love is patient, love is kind, and is not jealous; love does not brag and is not arrogant, does not act unbecomingly; it does not seek its own, is not provoked, does not take into account a wrong suffered, does not rejoice in unrighteousness, but rejoices with the truth; bears all things, believes all things, hopes all things, endures all things. Love never fails . . . (1 Cor. 13:4-8).

Here are some of the qualities contained in these verses, laid out on an imaginary cafeteria counter:

kindness	peace
tender-heartedness	thankfulness
forgiving	reasonableness
compassion	merciful
humility	unhypocritical
gentleness	not jealous or envious
patience	

Help yourself. It's all free. The more you take, the farther along you will be on your way to becoming indestructible.

8 / Your Inner Life: The Mind

8 / Your Inner Life: The Mind

THE INSIDE STORY /

The mind is the most private part of your inner life. No one can know for sure what you allow to enter into it, and no one can know what goes on in your mind unless you reveal it.

SECTION 1: MANAGING YOUR MIND /

The longer I work with people, the more convinced I become that everyone can and does control his mind. We make our own decisions, and no one can change them.

POWER TO CHOOSE /

Here are some areas in which you have the power to make choices:

1. Give an accurate report, inaccurate report, or no report when questioned.
2. Share all or part or nothing that is on your mind.
3. Choose to obey or disobey.
4. Obey outwardly and rebel inwardly.
5. Choose or refuse to study.
6. Look at whatever you choose to look at.
7. Choose what you will listen to, whether it involves people, radio, TV, records, movies, cassettes. If forced to listen, what you hear can surely "go in one ear and out the other."
8. Read or refuse to read whatever you wish.

9. Seek advice and then follow or ignore it.
10. Resist advice.
11. Turn away from past teaching or abide by it.
12. Make plans and carry them out, drop them, or change them.
13. Form your own opinions.
14. Forgive people.
15. Nurse your grudges.
16. Reveal or conceal feelings and emotions.
17. Turn to God or away from Him.

Everyone has the power of choice. While writing this chapter, I observed a tiny four-year-old refuse to eat his bread in spite of the threat of physical punishment at the hands of a 200-pound adult. He was prepared to risk a spanking, suffer hunger, and sacrifice the good will of his parents, but he wasn't eating that bread.

Recently, some friends were sharing experiences regarding their children and piano lessons. One child refused to practice no matter what incentives or threats were made. After three months, the parents gave up, worried about the future of their "bull-headed" child.

Another child in the same family also resisted practicing piano, but gave up easily. Her parents considered her a "more sensible" child than her brother. To their surprise, she quit playing the piano the day of high school graduation. When pressed for a reason, she explained she never liked it, but it wasn't worth the hassle to fight it. Their daughter wasn't as "sensible" as they thought she was.

TWO CHILDREN IN CONTROL OF THEIR CHOICES /

Here were two children with identical minds about practicing piano. They illustrate the difficulty we have in making judgments about someone's inner life based upon their words or behavior.

Both children were in charge of their own minds. In the boy's case, his words and behavior were a true reflection of what was on his mind. In the girl's case, her words and behavior were a misrepresentation of what was on her mind. The Bible puts it clearly:

For as he thinks within himself, so he is. He says to you, "Eat
and drink!" But his heart is not with you (Prov. 23:7).

Our reflection can be real—or an illusion of how
we really are.

WE DECIDE WHAT ENTERS OUT MINDS /

Last night, I was visiting a friend and noticed a
thick booklet lying on a table, entitled *Cessna 340 Manual*.
My friend explained that he was taking delivery on an
airplane and was cramming his head full of information
about the plane. Clearly, if he means to fly that plane safely,
he is wise to commit himself to obeying the instructions in
that manual.

My friend has the power to choose to study his
manual and fill his mind with airplane facts. A passenger on
a commercial airplane can also choose what to do with the
mind while in flight:

1. Choose a magazine.
2. Use earphones that plug into at least six
   channels for music or speeches.
3. Read material he brought on board.
4. Write reports, do planning, or other work.
5. Sit and think.
6. Engage in a conversation.
7. Watch the people around him.
8. Sleep.

MANY VOICES /

You are constantly exchanging ideas with
partners, parents, relatives, friends, teachers, preachers, and
others.

We are all familiar with the flood of ideas coming
at us from the radio, TV, newspapers, books, magazines,
pamphlets, movies, billboards, and advertisements.

What will you do with this mass of information
that bids for your attention? Remember, it's *your* attention.
It's *your* mind. There is no avoiding your responsibility.
There are several options open to you.

First, you have considerable choice of what you
will read, look at, or listen to.

Second, once your mind is exposed to this mass of

ideas, you must decide whether to accept or reject them. You may be well equipped or poorly equipped for the task, but no one can do it for you.

YOU NEED A FILTER /

You need a standard to go by. The Bible says:

> "My thoughts are not your thoughts, neither are your ways My ways," declares the LORD (Isa. 55:8).

Since our thoughts are not His thoughts, nor our ways His ways we need to make a conscious, deliberate effort to know Him. Just as my friend filled his mind with instructions from the *Cessna 340* manual in order to "fly right," so we must fill our head with God's commandments in order to think straight—to develop a basis for keeping acceptable ideas and filtering out the unacceptable ones. Kind David, a man after God's own heart, said of God's laws:

> The law of the LORD is perfect, restoring the soul; the testimony of the LORD is sure, making wise the simple. The precepts of the LORD are right, rejoicing the heart; The commandment of the LORD is pure, enlightening the eyes. The fear of the LORD is clean, enduring forever; the judgments of the LORD are true; they are righteous altogether. They are more desirable than gold, yes than much fine gold (Ps. 19:7-10).

Again, he says:

> The mouth of the righteous utters wisdom, and his tongue speaks justice. The law of his God is in his heart; his steps do not slip (Ps. 37:30-31).

> Let the words of my mouth and the meditation of my heart be acceptable in Thy sight, O LORD, my rock and my redeemer (Ps. 19:14).

> I have more insight than all my teachers, for Thy testimonies are my meditation (Ps. 119:99).

It is profitable for anyone to invest many hours in the study of the Proverbs. Here are some of them:

> If you cry for discernment, lift your voice for understanding: If you seek her as silver, and search for her as for hidden treasures; then you will discern the fear of the LORD, and discover the knowledge of God (Prov. 2:3-5).

> The fear of the LORD is to hate evil; pride and arrogance and

> the evil way, and the perverted mouth, I hate (Prov. 8:13).
>
> He who gets wisdom loves his own soul; he who keeps understanding will find good (Prov. 19:8).

This is no simple path to follow. The management of your mind is a daily task. It involves continuous study, and no one can do it for you. The apostle Paul gives us some instructions that are attainable by anyone who will pay the price. His advice demands a choice, and this choice must be renewed day by day:

> We are destroying speculations and every lofty thing raised up against the knowlege of God, and we are taking every thought captive to the obedience of Christ (2 Cor. 10:5).
>
> Do not be conformed to this world, but be transformed by the renewing of your mind, that you may prove what the will of God is, that which is good and acceptable and perfect (Rom. 12:2-3).

DECISION MAKING /

Every day of your life, you are called upon to make decisions, and you must respond to decisions other people make that affect you. Some decisions facing you are how to respond to tragedy, death, some event beyond your control, or a dirty trick.

This whole area of decision making is a common subject in the consulting room. Most of my clients who bring up this subject are anxious about a decision to be made or are disturbed and angry over the outcome of a decision or event that has already occurred, whether my client participated in it or was only affected by it.

Following are some Bible verses that have proven useful in managing the mental activity involved in decision making:

> Delight yourself in the LORD; and He will give you the desires of your heart. Commit your way to the LORD, trust also in Him, and He will do it. And He will bring forth your righteousness as the light, and your judgment as the noonday. Rest in the LORD and wait patiently for Him; fret not yourself because of him who prospers in his way, because of the man who carries out wicked schemes (Ps. 37:4-7).
>
> Commit your works to the LORD, and your plans will be established (Prov. 16:3).

> And we know that God causes all things to work together for good to those who love God, to those who are called according to His purpose (Rom. 8:28).

Some reflection on those verses makes it clear that we err if we try to evaluate the immediate outcome of a decision or event.

The emphasis in these verses is not on the outcome of the decisions, but on the attitude of the decision maker.

Delight yourself in the Lord.

Commit your way to the Lord.

Trust in Him.

Rest in the Lord.

Wait patiently for Him.

Fret not yourself.

God causes all things to work together for good for those who love Him.

LIFE'S A DRAMA . . . AND YOU'RE THE STAR! /

If you meet the conditions just mentioned, life will become more like watching a drama or a movie. You know before you begin watching that the script has already been written.

There will be happy times, crisis times, even tragic times. Part of the reason for watching is to enjoy the suspense and some of the emotion as the story line develops.

You will enjoy watching how things turn out. You won't be anxious about making plans or pursuing the desires of your heart. You know that His thoughts are not your thoughts, nor are His ways your ways. It's fun to see how close you can come to His plans and to see how all things work together for good.

Let me emphasize again that these verses stress the attitude of the decision maker rather than evaluate the immediate outcome of a decision or an event. It takes months or even years to see how all things work together.

I have stood by many people who have gone through crisis times. Everyone eventually sees his problem work out. Let me share one such story with you that covers a period of six years.

RONALD'S STORY /

Ronald was in his early 50s when his wife died in a car accident. There is no way to explain such a tragedy. Ronald was a man committed to trusting God, and his faith sustained him as he went through the process of building a new life.

Two years later, he accepted a job in another state. This meant selling his house, leasing an apartment in another state, and getting settled there. The new job never did work out, and after struggling with it for two years, he finally gave up.

This development seemed like such a needless event for a Christian who was committed to trusting and resting in God. His friends wondered why God was treating Ronald this way. He went on trusting, insisting that one of these days everything would make sense.

He found a job in another city, which meant another move. As it turned out, he fit that job like a hand and glove. Better yet, he found a circle of Christian friends with whom he was more compatible than any group of friends he ever had.

Another unexpected event happened to Ronald. A lovely Christian widow showed up seemingly out of nowhere. After a few months they announced their plans to get married. What a happy marriage it turned out to be!

This story is like thousands of others. The events of life are bittersweet. They make sense only over the long haul. If you were to ask Ronald what he thought about the Christian life, he would quote Romans 8:28 to you:

> We know that God causes all things to work together for good to those who love God, to those who are called according to His purpose.

RESULTS OF IGNORING GOD: DEPRAVED MINDS /

We live in a tension-filled world. Violence, deception, fraud, strained relations seem to be the norm rather than the exception.

A typical daily newspaper front page will include: (1) reports of some full-scale war somewhere in the world, (2) a local or area murder story, (3) fraudulent activity locally, (4) a kidnapping somewhere, (5) a local barroom brawl or some such story. When you think about the human relations you know of, don't they compare to the following?

> Just as they did not see fit to acknowledge God any longer, God gave them over to a depraved mind, to do those things which are not proper, being filled with all unrighteousness, wickedness, greed, malice; full of envy, murder, strife, deceit, malice; they are gossips, slanderers, haters of God, insolent, arrogant, boastful, inventors of evil, disobedient to parents, without understanding, untrustworthy, unloving, unmerciful (Rom. 1:28-31).

The way to keep from developing such a mind is to choose to know and keep God's commandments.

A HAPPIER NOTE: WHOLESOME MINDS /

The Bible verses in this chapter have been assembled with an emphasis on the management of your mind. You can choose what will linger there. You can have a depraved mind—or a wholesome mind. If you seek to please God with the use of your mind, you will be able to describe yourself as did the prophet Jeremiah:

> Thus says the LORD, "Let not a wise man boast of his wisdom, and let not the mighty man boast of his might, let not a rich man boast of his riches; but let him who boasts boast of this, that he understands and knows Me, that I am the LORD who exercises lovingkindness, justice, and righteousness on earth; for I delight in these things," declares the LORD (Jer. 9:23-24).

Finally, some classic advice from the apostle Paul on the management of your mind:

> Be anxious for nothing, but in everything by prayer and supplication with thanksgiving let your requests be made known to God. And the peace of God, which surpasses all comprehension, shall guard your hearts and minds in Christ Jesus. Finally, brethren, whatever is true, whatever is honorable, whatever is right, whatever is pure, whatever is lovely, whatever is of good repute, if there is any excellence and if anything worthy of praise, let your mind dwell on these things (Phil. 4:6-8).

SECTION 2: THE KEY TO FELLOWSHIP—
A MEETING OF THE MINDS /

Everyone interacts with other people—in a family,

at work, at church, in a store, in a car, in a neighborhood. In the process, you either reveal or conceal what is on your mind.

DECEPTION IS COMMON /

An anxious, disgruntled young man—married six months—came to see me about his marriage. He hated his wife's hairdo, her cooking, housekeeping, and love-making. What was he doing about it?

"I haven't the heart to tell her, Dr. Brandt. So I've been telling her what a good job she's been doing in each of those areas."

A very worried and tense young lady came to see me because her wedding date was two months away, and she couldn't stand her boyfriend. He was tied to his family, wasted his money, and didn't bathe often enough.

What was she doing about the problem? Nothing. Instead, she told him how much she loved and admired him and gave everyone the impression that she was thrilled about the upcoming marriage.

Another young lady came to see me because she disagreed constantly with her mother. What did she do about it? Obeyed outwardly and seethed with resentment inwardly.

Many of my clients appear to be radiantly happy when they enter the consulting room, but before the session is over they reveal a bitter, hateful spirit.

I have often been in social gatherings also attended by my clients. Some of the most bitter ones appear to be the happiest people there.

All these people were prepared to do anything to avoid the hatred, anger, ill will or the critical spirit of another person to be directed at them—even to the point of lying and deceiving.

Why?

Because their sense of self-respect depended on the good will of the other person.

But a deceitful relationship is self-defeating. These people didn't come to see me because the other person was dissatisfied. They came because they, themselves, were miserable.

In the courtroom, if a witness fails to reveal accurately what is on his mind, it is called perjury. The Watergate scandal should be a stark reminder of the misery we can cause ourselves by covering up the truth. The men involved brought the wrath of the nation down on themselves.

In day-to-day, human relations, we tend to create minor Watergates when we misrepresent what is on our minds and hearts. We can give ourselves a variety of reasons for practicing such deception. Some are:

1. My friend would hate me.
2. My mother would be upset.
3. My father would be angry.
4. My teacher would flunk me.
5. My boss would fire me.
6. My friends would be hurt or surprised.
7. My church would ask me to leave.

When you misrepresent yourself to others—that is, when you lie and deceive others, for any reason, you violate a commandment, which is:

> Laying aside falsehood, speak truth, each one of you, with his neighbor, for we are members of one another (Eph. 4:25).

To deceive another is to chip away at your own self-respect, even though you receive praise and good will as a result.

A REMINDER /

Love, joy, peace, patience, kindness, goodness, faithfulness, gentleness, and self-control are the fruit of the Spirit. These qualities exist only in a person who draws upon them from God.

They can be directed toward you only if the other person is rightly related to God.

If someone is nursing hatred or wrath in his heart and then discovers that he has been deceived, he will shower that wrath on whoever deceived him just as surely as the nation showered its wrath on the Watergate people.

You err when your sense of self-respect is based on the spiritual condition of another person. You build your own self-respect when your words, behavior, emotions, and mental activity line up with God's commandments.

OUR JUDGMENT OF PEOPLE IS LIMITED /

The Bible says:

> As in water face reflects face, so the heart of man reflects man (Prov. 27:19).

> The heart knows its own bitterness, and a stranger does not share its joy (Prov. 14:10).

Only you know what goes on underneath your skin. Whether bitterness or joy floods your soul is known only to you. I have spent a lifetime studying people, and am fully convinced that I cannot accurately decide what goes on in someone else's heart and mind. A person may look miserable but can be radiant on the inside. Another may look happy but can be miserable on the inside.

"I'LL THROW YOU INTO THE FURNACE!" /

A janitor walked in on a nursery school at his church. The children were working on cutouts: paper scraps littered the floor. Gruffly, he ordered:

"You kids clean up this paper, or I'll throw you into the furnace!"

The teacher, a newcomer in the church, gasped. But the children ran gleefully into his outstretched arms. They knew that all he meant was:

"Hello, kids, I'm glad to see you!"

From what the janitor said, the teacher got a totally wrong impression of his attitude toward children. I am impressed by the wisdom given to us by the apostle Paul:

> But you, why do you judge your brother? Or you again, why do you regard your brother with contempt? For we shall all stand before the judgment seat of God. For it is written, "As I live, says the LORD, every knee shall bow to Me, and every tongue shall give praise to God." So then each of us shall give account of himself to God. Therefore, let us not judge one another any more, but rather determine this—not to put an obstacle or a stumbling block in a brother's way (Rom. 14:10-13).

You can hear what I say and observe what I do, but you can't judge the accuracy of what I say, nor can you judge my motives or my sincerity.

What you can do is *judge the accuracy of what you say and your own motives and sincerity.* You and I must stand or fall before God alone, when it comes to our mental activity. How, then, can we know each other? Only as we choose to open our minds and hearts to one another.

THE BASIS FOR FELLOWSHIP /

The Bible says:

> Now I exhort you, brethren, by the name of our Lord Jesus Christ, that you all agree, and there be no divisions among you, but you be made complete in the same mind and in the same judgment (1 Cor. 1:10).

> If therefore there is any encouragement in Christ, if there is any consolation of love, if there is any fellowship of the Spirit, if any affection and compassion, make my joy complete by being of the same mind, maintaining the same love, united in spirit, intent on one purpose (Phil. 2:1-2).

LIKE-MINDED /

Contained in the verses mentioned above is a description of the mental activity involved in maintaining fellowship.

	agreement
Like-minded	no divisions
	same mind
	same judgment
	same love
	one purpose

If your minds are not together, your are not together, even if you speak the same words and do the same things. To illustrate, look at these little doodles:

I like your hairdo.

Your cooking is great!

Obviously, his mind agrees with his words. He is communicating accurately.

Here is another illustration:

He and she were both hungry and agreed to go out. She said she would go anywhere, but she didn't mean it and admitted it.

He agreed verbally to go to the Steak House, but he didn't change his feelings. To that extent, he deceived her, and they were not like-minded.

What should he have done? He could have said:

"I'd rather not go to the Steak House but I will."

Why is that so important? He is telling the truth, rather than deceiving her.

INVISIBLE BURDEN /

Audrey was known as a good neighbor, a cheerful wife, and a generous, considerate person who loved to go out of her way to be helpful.

Ralph was proud of his cheerful, neighborly wife, who never fussed at him, even when he brought guests home on short notice.

In the consulting room, she said:

"I'm a very unhappy person. I came to find out why." These little drawings give the reason:

She

I'd be glad to entertain your guests.

She

So glad to have you over after church.

Isn't it strange that Audrey was more concerned about appearing to be cheerful and generous than really being cheerful and generous?

This intelligent woman didn't seem to realize the difference between acting and being real. Her invisible, but very heavy, burden was *self-centeredness and deception.* She called it neighborliness and cooperation. How true these verses are:

> The heart is more deceitful than all else and is desperately sick; who can understand it? I, the LORD, search the heart, I test the mind, even to give to each man according to his ways (Jer. 17:9-10).

Like so many of us, all Audrey needed was some instruction. No one needed to tell her that all her hard work only produced more personal misery. She saw where she was wrong and asked God to replace her selfish, deceitful spirit with His spirit of truth and service. Put in a Bible verse:

> The goal of our instruction is love from a pure heart and a good conscience and a sincere faith (1 Tim. 1:5).

Then she worked out a more realistic schedule with her husband and neighbors. This was not as easy as it sounds.

First, she had to admit to Ralph that much of her friendly cooperation was just plain phoniness. He didn't take it very well at first, but it was true, and he had to live with it.

Second, they needed to negotiate a new plan. This wasn't easy either. Ralph was so accustomed to Audrey's agreeing with everything, he had to get used to contrary opinions coming from her. Ralph, in the past, could easily get his own opinion accepted, it seemed, but now he frequently heard her say:

"You haven't changed my mind." That was a stopper when they came to a deadlock.

Third, they had to learn to settle deadlocks—that is, making decisions knowing that their opinions differed. In such cases, one of them had to make the decision, and the other had to concede.

In the long run, Audrey and Ralph built a good marriage on the firm foundation of truth.

GETTING YOUR MINDS TOGETHER /

> . . . being of the same mind, maintaining the same love, united in spirit, intent on one purpose (Phil. 2:2).

If your minds are not together, you are not together. I recall meeting a man at a conference who was talked into attending against his will. He was there in body but not in mind and left in two days.

A lady told me how she despised the dress she was wearing. She hated the color, but her husband made her wear it.

A man suffered agony sitting in church every Sunday morning. He was there bodily to get his wife off his back, but his mind wasn't there.

These people illustrate the struggle that goes on in our minds. If fellowship is the goal, this mental conflict must cease. There are a variety of ways to come to a meeting of minds:

1. Agreement
2. Concession
3. Compromise
4. Acceptance of authority

AGREEMENT /

When two or more people decide to drive to New York next Tuesday and stay at a certain Holiday Inn for a week—and there are no mental reservations—this could be called an agreement.

CONCESSION /

If someone in the party prefers a Sheraton Inn, but finally agrees to the Holiday Inn, this is a concession—provided the decision is made without mental reservations.

COMPROMISE /

On the way to New York, the travelers take turns driving. One drives 50 mph, the other 70 mph. One's speed is too slow to suit the other, and the other's speed is too fast for his partner. So, they agree to both drive 60 mph. This is a compromise.

ACCEPTANCE OF AUTHORITY /

The travelers differ over how often to stop along the way and where to eat. Finally, they agree that there must be a leader who has the last word, and one of them is chosen to be the leader.

The leader decides to give the traveling partner the responsibility for deciding where to eat. The leader will decide when to stop. This is accepting authority.

NEGOTIATION INVOLVES THE EMOTIONS AND ATTITUDES /

No person can separate feelings, thoughts, and actions as we have done in this book. This is especially true when differences of opinion arise. We all tend to go our own way, and our opinions will sooner or later collide with someone else's. So to work on being like-minded is a continuous process, and the process will reveal the spirit.

THE NEWLYWEDS /

Two newlyweds plan on both working. But the wife gets pregnant, so they must revise their plans. They are finally accustomed to her pregnancy when she has the baby, which calls for new plans again. About the time they adjust to the baby it is now a toddler, which requires more shifts in plans.

So it goes all our lives. There are constant changes forcing us to make adjustments—all requiring daily decisions. The necessity for making all these decisions calls for a certain attitude as described by this verse:

> Do nothing from selfishness or empty conceit, but with humility of mind let each of you regard one another as more important than himself (Phil. 2:3).

Negotiating new agreements can be fun only if you approach one another unselfishly, humbly, and keep the importance of the other person in mind.

When there is a difference of opinion and you are not walking in the Spirit, it is easy to lose sight of the importance of the other person and become preoccupied with the negative side of the person you are negotiating with.

In marriage counseling, I have observed that a young couple, contemplating marriage, can't say enough good about the partner, who has become the most important person in the world.

But in the consulting room, because they are no longer like-minded, all they can think of is what's wrong with the partner. This negative way of thinking can happen whenever there is a clash of opinion, even though the qualities of the opponent are still there.

CONSIDER BOTH SIDES /

> Do not merely look out for your own personal interests, but also for the interests of others (Phil. 2:4).

In the effort to come to a meeting of minds, you tend to get caught up in your own interest and lose sight of the other person's. Remember, to come to a meeting of minds implies a difference of opinion in the first place.

TO DRAPE OR NOT TO DRAPE /

Recently, we moved to a home which had a large picture window overlooking some water. Eva wanted drapes on the window, and I didn't. We discussed the issue back and forth.

She even proved to me that everyone we knew had drapes on their windows. After everything that could be said on both sides was said, she still wanted drapes, and I didn't. A decision had to be made. Being the head of the family, it was my decision. The result?

We now have drapes.

Why?

Eva spends more time in that home than I do. I want to please her, and she wants drapes. Since it's only a matter of opinion, and considering her interests as well as mine, the drapes didn't affect the view, so it just made sense to yield to her interest. That settled it. We came to a meeting of minds.

THE SPIRIT OF A SERVANT /

> Have this attitude in yourselves which was also in Christ Jesus, who, although He existed in the form of God, did not regard equality with God a thing to be grasped, but emptied Himself, taking the form of a bondservant, and being made in the likeness of men. And being found in appearance as a man, He humbled Himself by becoming obedient to the point of death, even death on a cross (Phil. 2:5-8).

Such is the attitude of a servant toward whomever is served. Jesus was someone—the Son of God, the creator of the universe. Yet, He gave Himself fully to His task. He didn't need to. He just surrendered Himself.

YOU ARE SOMEONE /

You are also someone, with talent, ability, creativity, training. You have power, influence, perhaps riches. You may be smarter than the person you are negotiating with.

I used to think that servants are people who have lowly positions with low pay. When I was a boy my mother would take in washings and scrub floors. I would deliver the washings to these huge homes. There were maids, cooks, chauffeurs, gardeners. In my youthful mind, these people were servants.

Now, I see it differently. Physicians, teachers, counselors, lawyers, builders, and bankers are servants, too. They make lots of money. It's not the pay that makes you a servant. It's the giving of yourself totally to your task.

It is this spirit that is required if you are to be like-minded. You give yourself totally and completely to find a basis for a meeting of minds with whomever you must cooperate.

Training, ability, power, or wealth does not exempt you from making a continuous effort to maintain like-mindedness—even unto death.

A good example is a football player. He undergoes rigorous training, suffers pain, and risks injury to carry out his commitment to his team.

SUMMARY /

The management of your mind is your responsibility. No one can do it for you. If you use God's commandments as a standard for what you allow into your mind, and if you commit yourself to speak the truth and to be like-minded with the people in your life, you will build your own self-respect and self-love and you will be on the road to being indestructible.

9 / Your Inner Life: Goals

9 / Your Inner Life: Goals

GOALS BRING LIFE INTO FOCUS /

I'm firmly convinced that the goals we set for ourselves account for one of the most crucial factors of all in building our self-respect or self-love.

Goals bring life into focus. They give meaning and purpose to life.

ASSAULT ON MT. WHITNEY /

I have a friend who was determined to climb Mt. Whitney, which is the tallest mountain in the continental United States—more than 14,000 feet high. He invited me to go along.

It is a long, hard, two-day climb. Each person has to carry a heavy backpack with two days of food, extra clothing in case it rains or snows, a sleeping bag, and a tank of oxygen.

The day came when we stood at the foot of the trail, thrilled as we looked up and saw the peak high up in the sky.

We had many trails ahead of us. There were long, easy sections. There were fast-moving mountain streams. Also ahead were long, steep climbs that left our muscles aching and our lungs panting for breath.

Toward the end of the first day, the shrubbery and grass began to disappear and we had left the tall trees behind. There were rocks and some small, gnarled, tough, little trees.

As we looked up, the peak seemed as far away as ever.

A HARD NIGHT'S SLEEP /

We stopped for the night and removed our packs from our weary backs. There was a cold, biting wind blowing. We built a fire, heated up some soup, and sat back to enjoy the breath-taking scenery. We didn't mind the aching muscles. We accepted the pain and the cold as a part of reaching our goal.

Finally, we rolled out our sleeping bags, crawled in, and tried to sleep on the hard rocks with a howling wind blowing that made us huddle as far down as possible in our sleeping bags.

In the morning, when we crawled out of our bags, our bones ached from spending the night on that hard rock, and our muscles ached from yesterday's climb, but we were happy and wouldn't have wanted it any other way.

After a breakfast of dried meat and peanuts, we hoisted our packs up on our aching backs and started out. The trail became steeper and steeper.

IT FOOLS YOU /

Many times at the foot of a long, steep climb, it looked like we had finally reached the peak. But when we reached the top, we discovered that there were more peaks beyond. We climbed down, up, down, up. The air became very thin, and we had to breathe oxygen from our little tank in order to keep going.

Those little peaks seemed to keep coming forever.

Climbing those lesser peaks made sense only because we kept that final peak in view. Finally, after some eight hours of climbing, sometimes through deep snow banks, and seemingly having expended every ounce of energy, we stood on the peak, 14,000 feet up—with a breath-taking 360° view to enjoy.

Our long-range goal of reaching the peak gave meaning to subjecting ourselves to the expenditure of energy, pain, sleeping on a hard rock, eating coarse food, and lugging a heavy pack on our backs. It was an exhilarating, rewarding experience. High up on the peak of Mt. Whitney, we vowed to climb some other mountains—which we have done.

A LONG-RANGE GOAL GIVES MEANING TO LIFE /

The Bible says:

> For we must all appear before the judgment seat of Christ, that each one may be recompensed for his deeds done in the body, according to what he has done, whether good or bad (2 Cor. 5:10).

In the long run, we will all see Jesus and give account of how we managed these bodies of ours. He has given us instructions for living, and we will be evaluated on the basis of them. We will do well to prepare for that day.

GIVING ACCOUNT /

A few years ago, I received an official-looking envelope in the mail. It was from the United States Government, inviting me to appear before the Internal Revenue Service to give account of what I had done with my money for the three previous years.

There was nothing to fear, because I had retained the services of a competent CPA who had guided me across the years in properly accounting for the use of my money and paying taxes as necessary.

After a very thorough review, the IRS announced that we had made some errors and were entitled to a $500 refund.

So it will be when we stand before the judgment seat of Christ. There is nothing to fear if we have managed our lives as He instructed us. Be assured that we will be judged according to His commandments.

When Moses died, it is recorded that God gave Joshua some specific instructions as he took over the leadership of the Israelites:

> Only be strong and very courageous; be careful to do according to all the law which Moses My servant commanded you; do not turn from it to the right or to the left, so that you may have success wherever you go (Josh. 1:7).

King Solomon, who tried everything under the

sun, came to the following conclusion:

> The conclusion, when all has been heard, is: fear God and keep His commandments, because this applies to every person. Because God will bring every act to judgment, everything which is hidden, whether it is good or evil (Eccl. 12:13-14).

In his first letter to Timothy, the apostle Paul advised:

> Be diligent to present yourself approved to God as a workman who does not need to be ashamed, handling accurately the word of truth (2 Tim. 2:15).

The central theme of this book is knowing and obeying God's commandments. One reason for this emphasis is the fact that one day we will be judged according to them.

In the meantime, keeping them leads to joy and blessing. They keep us from stumbling, give insight and understanding of righteousness, and will make our way prosperous and help us to have good success. For the long run, here is a good goal:

> Set your mind on the things above, not on the things that are on the earth (Col. 3:2).

EARTHBOUND GOALS LEAD TO FRUSTRATION /

Robert Burns penned some insightful lines many years ago:

> But pleasures are like poppies spread—
> You seize the flower, its bloom is shed.

We tend to get involved with people, activities, and things with a great surge of energy and pleasurable expectations.

I once watched in amazement as a young lady who had gained weight steadily, suddenly proceeded to shed twenty-five pounds.

Why?

She was to be a bridesmaid in a wedding. After the wedding, her weight started to climb again.

A boy who aimlessly spent his allowance on bubble gum, candy, or gadgets for his bicycle suddenly was interested in all the odd jobs he could get so he could save his money.

Why?

His father said he could buy a car.

We all know of young men who were normally careless about their appearance but who became eager to bathe, comb their hair, or wear a suit. They became interested in a particular girl.

We watch people who "fall in love" suddenly go places and do things that no one could have forced them into.

We watch people work two jobs, stop spending money on clothes, drive a cheaper car, or do anything else if they decide to save for college, or to get married, or to buy a house.

In airports, we can see eager people waiting for the arrival of a plane. They pace up and down, eyes shining, highly elated. When the expected person shows up, they get all excited, clap their hands, jump up and down, fly into each other's arms, hug and kiss, oblivious to anyone else around them, and walk arm in arm toward the baggage claim area eagerly talking together.

Anticipation fans our expectations. Our hope is that reaching an objective will result in great satisfaction and pleasure. Then, after several months or years of effort, we end up disillusioned.

Many people have made plenty of money but have no good reason for spending it. Shopping malls are full of people aimlessly wandering from store to store, not looking for anything in particular, perhaps ending up eating something or buying something they don't need.

Others have developed their talent and ability and now have no desire to use it. Many people approach me these days about changing careers. They have learned a trade or a profession, but receive no satisfaction from their work, even though they are using their talent and the pay is good.

Some people can't wait to retire so they can pursue a life of leisure, yet thousands of them, retired and on a good pension plan, are hopelessly bored with luxury and ease.

There are many surprises for a counselor. For instance, a very unhappy man asked me for counsel. He had nothing to live for. What made this a particularly pathetic case was the fact that he was a multimillionaire, owned more than a dozen manufacturing plants, and had hundreds of employees.

He was a rabid student of management, and had all the duties and responsibilities related to his business delegated to competent, highly trained people.

Why, then, would he show up in a counselor's office? He had delegated himself into uselessness. No one needed him. He was lost without his responsibilities and bored without them.

Many beautiful, healthy, affectionate people end up in the consulting room because there is no one they want to please or respond to. Marriage has turned to ashes.

Family life doesn't satisfy, they say. I came across some chilling statistics that reflect the aimless, goal-less society we live in. These were compiled a few years ago in a report entitled "Growing Up Forgotten":

1. There were more than one million divorces in 1976.
2. There were more than one million legal abortions in 1976.
3. There were more than one million children who were victims of child abuse or neglect in 1976.
4. Suicide has become the fifth leading cause of death among adolescents.
5. Children under fifteen are the only age group that has recently shown an increase in admission rates to mental hospitals.
6. Crime and violence among young teen-agers in the streets and in the schools is on the rise.
7. An estimated one youth in nine and one male youth in six will be referred to juvenile court before eighteen.
8. There were more than one million teen-age runaways in 1976.

Couples are abandoning marriage and their families by the droves. The demands of the relationship are too great, so either the husband or wife lashes out at the other or just walks away and abandons the whole thing.

GOOD GOALS DON'T SATISFY /

I have described some goals that should have satisfied, but they didn't. Let me list some:

1. Making money
2. Acquiring things
3. Building your own business
4. Retiring with a good pension
5. A trim figure
6. Using talent and ability
7. Marriage
8. Parenthood

These are all good goals. Everyone must make a living and provide for his future. We all need to do what is necessary to maintain health and use our own talents and abilities. Who would quarrel with having marriage and a happy family life as a goal? Surely everyone who has worked until age sixty-five or seventy is entitled to an easy retirement.

Isn't it strange that after years of sincere effort pursuing good goals multitudes of people still end up in the consulting room looking for meaning and purpose in life? I am reminded of what King Solomon said:

> I have seen all the works which have been done under the sun, and behold, all is vanity and striving after wind (Eccl. 1:14).

> And I have seen that every labor and every skill which is done is the result of rivalry between a man and his neighbor. This too is vanity and striving after wind (Eccl. 4:4).

His gloomy conclusions have a strangely modern ring to them. I hear almost the same words in the consulting room:

"I'm fed up with competing."

"I end up frustrated after all these years of hard work."

"I've poured my life into this family and nobody cares."

Doing good things all your life is like climbing a steep section of a mountain trail. It only gives you aching muscles unless you keep the peak in mind.

Doing good things only gives meaning and purpose if in the doing of them you keep the real long-range goal in mind.

> For we must all appear before the judgment seat of Christ, that each one may be recompensed for his deeds in the body, according to what he has done, whether good or bad (2 Cor. 5:10).

This will be a great day if you have kept the greatest commandment of all:

> You shall love the Lord your God with all your heart, and with all your soul, and with all your mind (Matt. 22:37).

If you love Him that much, you will have done as Jesus asked us to do:

> If you love Me, you will keep My commandments (John 14:15).

If you know and keep the commandments, it means that in the process of making a living, making money, acquiring an estate, using your talent, keeping fit, maintaining a marriage and a family, you do it all in a way that pleases Jesus, whom you love and who one day will evaluate you.

If your behavior, your conversation, your reactions, your mind, and your goals are pleasing in His sight, the day-by-day duties will have meaning and purpose.

YOUR LONG-RANGE GOAL GIVES PERSPECTIVE TO LIFE /

> The day of the Lord will come like a thief, in which the heavens will pass away with a roar and the elements will be destroyed with intense heat, and the earth and its works will be burned up (2 Peter 3:10).

I was reading this verse one time while preparing for an overseas trip. At the time, I was a partner in a chain of eight large restaurants. I visited them all before leaving, which was a long, tiring chore.

The thought occurred to me then that it doesn't make sense to put your heart into something that eventually will be destroyed. I could picture all eight of those restaurants going up in smoke. No wonder riches don't satisfy. We all sense, at least vaguely, that things are temporary.

A few years ago, I was a partner in an apartment-house project. At the time we had the roof on and the doors and windows were installed in a three-story building containing twelve apartment units.

That night a strong wind blew down that building. As I studied the wreckage, it was as though an audible voice was telling me not to put my hopes in buildings. They are a puff of wind . . . or an earth tremor . . . or a touch of fire away from being destroyed.

Why should things like this happen? Perhaps to tell us to review our goals. Jesus said:

> Do not lay up for yourselves treasures upon earth, where moth and rust destroy, and where thieves break in and steal. But lay up for yourselves treasures in heaven, where neither moth nor rust destroys, and where thieves do not break in or steal; for where your treasure is, there will your heart be also (Matt. 6:19-21).
>
> What does it profit a man to gain the whole world, and forfeit his soul? (Mark 8:36).

Granted, everyone must make a living. In the process, we acquire wealth. If we follow the laws of economics carefully, we can acquire great wealth in the same amount of time that someone else barely ekes out a living. The futility of it is not the possession of wealth; it's putting our whole heart and soul into something that will eventually be destroyed.

What, then, is important? The Bible says:

> Since all these things are to be destroyed in this way, *what sort of people ought you to be* in holy conduct and godliness (2 Peter 3:11).

A SHORT-RANGE GOAL /

What sort of person ought we to be? When we meet Jesus, we will be evaluated on the basis of our "deeds done in the body, according to what you have done, whether good or bad" (2 Cor. 5:10)

Everyone must live out life every day. How should we conduct ourselves in the process? Look at some Bible verses:

Not every one who says to Me, "Lord, Lord," will enter the kingdom of heaven; but he who does the will of My Father who is in heaven (Matt. 7:21).

If any man is willing to do His will, he shall know of the teaching, whether it is of God, or whether I speak from Myself (John 7:17).

Seek first His kingdom and His righteousness; and all these things shall be added to you (Matt. 6:33).

For the kingdom of God is not eating and drinking, but righteousness and peace and joy in the Holy Spirit. For he who in this way serves Christ is acceptable to God and approved of men (Rom. 14:17-18).

He has told you, O man, what is good; and what does the LORD require of you but to do justice, to love kindness, and to walk humbly with your God (Micah 6:8).

Who may ascend into the hill of the LORD? And who may stand in His holy place? He who has clean hands and a pure heart, who has not lifted up his soul to falsehood, and has not sworn deceitfully (Ps. 24:3-4).

What credit is there if, when you sin and are harshly treated, you endure it with patience? But if when you do what is right and suffer for it you patiently endure it, this finds favor with God. For you have been called for this purpose, since Christ also suffered for you, leaving you an example for you to follow in His steps, who committed no sin, nor was any deceit found in His mouth; and while being reviled, He did not revile in return; while suffering, He uttered no threats, but kept entrusting Himself to Him who judges righteously (1 Peter 2:20-23).

The Creator of the universe is interested in what manner of person we are. These are the qualities important to Him as we go about our daily tasks:

    righteousness and peace and joy in the Holy Spirit
    justice
    kindness
    walking humbly with God
    clean hands
    a pure heart
    honesty
    being able to take mistreatment patiently.

Looking at life from God's viewpoint, these verses make sense:

> Watch over your heart with all diligence, for from it flow the springs of life (Prov. 4:23).
>
> Create in me a clean heart, O God, and renew a steadfast spirit within me (Ps. 51:10).

GOD'S WILL—TRUST HIM /

We say that life is enjoyable if all is peaceful in the marriage and family, we are well housed and well clothed, no conflicts are present on the job and with neighbors, we have no financial problems, all is well at work, we have ample income, and the weather is good.

Then, there are those times, we say, that take our joy away—like disagreements with our marriage partner, trouble with the children, illness, death, going broke, problems at work, getting fired, dirty tricks. If our hope for joy depends on things turning out right, then we are thinking earthly.

This next group of verses indicate that God wants us to entrust the people in our lives and the events of our lives into His hands. We can do everything possible to make things come out as we judge they should knowing, however, that our thoughts are not His thoughts, neither are our ways His ways. These verses indicate a commitment in advance of accepting whatever happens as from His hands:

> Trust in the LORD with all your heart, and do not lean on your own understanding. In all your ways acknowledge Him, and He will make your paths straight (Prov. 3:5-6).
>
> The LORD will continually guide you, and satisfy your desire in scorched places, and give strength to your bones; and you will be like a watered garden, and like a spring of water whose waters do not fail (Isa. 58:11).
>
> I have learned to be content in whatever circumstances I am. I know how to get along with humble means, and I also know how to live in prosperity; in any and every circumstance I have learned the secret of being filled and going hungry, both of having abundance and suffering need. I can do all things through Him who strengthens me (Phil. 4:11-13).
>
> But as for me, I trust in Thee, O LORD; I say, "Thou art my God." My times are in Thy hand (Ps. 31:14).
>
> In God I have put my trust, I shall not be afraid. What can man do to me? (Ps. 56:11).

> Cast your burden upon the LORD, and He will sustain you; He will never allow the righteous to be shaken (Ps. 55:22).

> Who is among you that fears the LORD, that obeys the voice of His servant, that walks in darkness and has no light? Let him trust in the name of the LORD and rely on His God (Isa. 50:10).

Life doesn't always make sense. I recently talked with a lady, age thirty-two, who lost her eyesight at age sixteen. Another lady in her early 40s, seriously crippled with rheumatoid arthritis, told me of her husband walking out on her.

My friend's twenty-four-year-old son died unexpectedly. Another good friend lost a daughter in a collision. Yesterday, I heard about another friend, in his early 50s, who slumped down into his chair and died.

I'm constantly hearing about crisis experiences that parents are having with their children.

This is the stuff of life. I have a long list of questions to ask Jesus when I see Him. In the meantime—I trust Him. You do the same.

WHEN THE CRISIS COMES . . . /

Before the crisis comes, when all is peaceful, you can commit your ways and your loved ones into His hands. You can do as those verses say:

> Learn to be content in whatever circumstances come along . . .

> Put your times in His hands . . .

> You will not fear what men can do to you . . .

> Let Him sustain you . . .

> When you walk in darkness, rely on God . . .

It's not a question of *if* some crisis will come. It's a matter of *when* it comes. You will be ready. A football player know there will be painful physical contact in the next game. So he gets his body ready. You know there is a crisis down the road. So get ready. As Jesus said:

> These things I have spoken to you, that in Me you may have peace. In the world you have tribulation, but take courage; I have overcome the world (John 16:33).

GOD'S WILL—TO SERVE /

> And He summoned the multitude with His disciples, and said to them, "If anyone wishes to come after Me, let him deny himself, and take up his cross, and follow Me. For whoever wishes to save his life shall lose it; and whoever loses his life for My sake and the gospel's shall save it. For what does it profit a man to gain the whole world, and forfeit his soul? (Mark 8:34-36).

The older we get, the more of this world's things we accumulate, the more acclaim comes our way, the more we realize that there is an emptiness to it all.

Jesus gives us the reason here.

All such activity is marginal in His sight. We find ourselves by losing ourselves in working for His sake and the gospel's.

James and John, two of Jesus' disciples, once came to Him with this request:

> "Teacher, we want You to do for us whatever we ask of You." And He said to them, "What do you want Me to do for You?" And they said to Him: "Grant that we may sit in Your glory, one on Your right, and one on Your left" (Mark 10:35-37).

That's long-range planning. They were applying for two key positions in heaven. Jesus explained that He did not have the authority to grant that request. When the rest of the disciples heard about it, they began to feel indignant toward James and John.

Then Jesus called all the disciples to Him. Instead of reprimanding James and John, as the disciples may have done, He told them *how to be first*. His instructions are most surprising to me. He said:

> . . . whoever wishes to become great among you shall be your servant; and whoever wishes to be first among you shall be slave of all. For even the Son of Man did not come to be served, but to serve, and to give His life a ransom for many (Mark 10:43-45).

The spirit of a servant.

The happy physician, dentist, counselor, lawyer, builder, banker, husband, wife, father, or mother is the one who gives himself completely to the task. There may be rewards or there may not be. There may be appreciation or there may not be. A servant doesn't perform services for rewards or appreciation. He serves in Jesus' name and for His sake. He gives because he is a servant.

SUMMARY /

Everyone must make a living, provide for the future, maintain health, use his talents and abilities, associate with family and friends.

Doing these things causes a weariness of the flesh, unless he sets proper goals.

LONG-RANGE GOAL /

> We must all appear before the judgment seat of Christ, that each one may be recompensed for his deeds in the body, according to what he has done, whether good or bad (2 Cor. 5:10).

We will anticipate this event as eagerly as people greeting one another in an airport if we have the right short-range goals.

Trust Him to guide you to people and events in life.

SHORT-RANGE GOALS /

1. Grow in your knowledge of the commandments.

2. Live righteously, peacefully, justly, love kindness, have a pure heart, take mistreatment patiently.

3. Trust God to guide you—trust Him to bring people and events into and out of your life.

4. Have the spirit of a servant—to serve rather than be served—to lose your life for Jesus' sake and the gospel's.

> To sum up, let all be harmonious, sympathetic, brotherly, kindhearted, and humble in spirit; not returning evil for evil, or insult for insult, but giving a blessing instead; for you were called for the very purpose that you might inherit a blessing (1 Peter 3:8-9).

If you accept these goals, your life will have meaning and purpose, and you will be on the way to becoming indestructible.

10 / Building Self-respect in Marriage

10 / Building Self-respect in Marriage

MANAGING YOUR ATTITUDE TOWARD YOUR MARRIAGE PARTNER /

There is no one person as intimately involved in your life as your marriage partner. So, your partner will make you more conscious of your inner life than anyone else. The Bible says:

> . . . a man shall leave his father and mother, and shall cleave to his wife; and they shall become one flesh (Gen. 2:24).

Your loyalty to one another, then, will build your self-respect. On the other hand, disloyalty to one another will chip away at your self-respect.

With your partner in mind, consider these verses:

> But now you also, put them all aside: anger, wrath, malice, slander, and abusive speech from your mouth. Do not lie to one another, since you laid aside the old self with its evil practices, and have put on the new self who is being renewed to a true knowledge according to the image of the One who created him (Col. 3:8-10).

If this is a picture of your inner life, you can keep it to yourself, but you are deceiving your partner, whose presence will be a continuous reminder to you of what you are doing.

Obviously, your self-respect will erode and your partner will have no idea of what is going on inside you. To give expression to such a spirit is equally demoralizing. It is not hard to understand why eventually such a person would flee from the marriage.

On the other hand, with your partner in mind, consider these verses:

> Put on a heart of compassion, kindness, humility, gentleness and patience; bearing with one another, and forgiving each other, whoever has a complaint against any one; just as the Lord forgave you, so also should you (Col. 3:12-13).

Clearly, if this is the condition of your inner life, the marriage relationship builds your self-respect.

The management of your inner life is your problem, discussed in detail in chapter 8.

COOPERATION /

> . . . be subject to one another in the fear of Christ (Eph. 5:21).

The will to cooperate is an important key to building self-respect. Competition between partners will have the opposite effect.

Cooperation implies that both husband and wife make the decision to dedicate time and effort in developing a mutually agreeable way of life.

Regular formal or informal conferences need to be held to assign responsibilities and develop policies, procedures, and rules that both can live with.

These little meetings can be held in the car, the kitchen, the living room—anywhere.

Two attitudes must exist in these meetings: (1) you mean to serve your partner, and (2) you will be bound by the decisions made by the partnership.

Daily effort, constant examination, and frequent changes will keep your relationship going.

The overriding spirit in all of this is to do it as unto the Lord. The Bible says:

> I exhort you, brethren, by the name of the Lord Jesus Christ, that you all agree, and there be no divisions among you, but you be made complete in the same mind and in the same judgment (1 Cor. 1:10).

Your self-respect will grow if you maintain an attitude of cooperation in the marriage—whether your partner does or not.

SUBMISSION /

No matter how committed you are to cooperate, it is inevitable that sooner or later you will become dead-locked over some decision. There is a way to settle a dead-lock if you are committed to resolve the divisions between you.

Someone must have the last word.

In a business, it's the president. In sports, it's the coach. In a game, it's the captain. In a marriage, it's the husband. The Bible says:

> Wives, be subject to your own husbands, as to the Lord (Eph. 5:22).

In the decision-making process, the wife should participate vigorously and forthrightly in the search for a mutually agreeable solution. The husband should think twice, or more, before going against his wife's judgment.

If the wife still disagrees with her husband's tie-breaking decision, she should say so.

The husband has two options when there is a deadlock:

1. Make the decision himself.
2. Ask his wife to make it.

Once done, both husband and wife submit to the decision and do all in their power to make it work.

Whether husband or wife, a spirit of submission builds self-respect. On the other hand, a spirit of selfishness or rebellion will chip away at self-respect.

COMMITMENT /

> Husbands, love your wives, just as Christ also loved the church and gave Himself up for her (Eph. 5:25).

As I travel around the country, I am appalled at the number of men who are walking away from their marriages and calling it quits. Granted, many of their wives have worked hard to make life miserable for these men.

If a man approaches his responsibility to marriage as Christ did toward the church, then the man will be committed until death. He will submit to the responsibility for maintaining a wholesome relationship with his wife.

There may be a period of time—perhaps years—when he has no choice but to stand by a totally rebellious, obnoxious, rejecting, or immoral woman, whose behavior is not worthy of his loyalty. His self-respect will remain intact if he retains the will to make it work, even though all his efforts are rejected.

Conversely, the behavior of many husbands can be totally obnoxious, mean, self-centered, even immoral. They may make no effort to be responsible husbands. They may totally reject any responsibility for the marriage. Yet, the will to stay committed will sustain a woman's self-respect.

> . . . you wives, be submissive to your own husbands so that even if any of them are disobedient to the word, they may be won without a word by the behavior of their wives, as they observe your chaste and respectful behavior (1 Peter 3:1-2).

The key in either case depends on a higher commitment:

. . . in the fear of Christ

. . . as to the Lord

. . . as Christ loved the church and gave Himself for it.

SEXUAL RESPONSIBILITY /

Sexual response dies when there are deadlocks and ill-will between the partners. Accordingly, when you do not respond to one another, look elsewhere for the reason.

There is a specific directive in the Bible to guide you in managing your physical relations:

> The wife does not have authority over her own body, but the husband does; and likewise the husband does not have authority over his own body, but the wife does. Stop depriving one another, except by agreement for a time that you may devote yourself to prayer, and come together again lest Satan tempt you because of your lack of self-control (1 Cor. 7:4-5).

Clearly, your partner's wish is your commandment. Obviously, the spirit here is one of mutual concern for one another.

To deprive your partner is to chip away at your

self-respect. To cooperate with your partner is to build your self-respect.

SUMMARY /

Marriage, like no other human relationship, will keep you up to date on the condition of your inner life. It is a personal decision, unrelated to marriage, whether or not you repent of a negative inner life, and allow God to flood your soul with His Spirit.

You build your own self-respect or self-love as you remain loyal, cooperative, submissive, and committed unto death to do all in your power to make the marriage work.

The key to maintaining such a spirit depends on a higher commitment:

As unto the Lord!

NOTE: The material in this chapter is based on the book, *I Want My Marriage to Be Better* (Zondervan), by the same authors.

11 / Building Self-respect as a Parent

11 / Building Self-respect as a Parent

MANAGING YOUR ATTITUDE TOWARD YOUR CHILDREN /

If your marriage partner is more intimately involved in your life than anyone else, your children run a close second. If marriage keeps you up to date on your spiritual condition, so will your children.

You will either reveal or conceal your spirit around your children. If there is anger, wrath, or malice in your heart, children will likely bring it out of you in the form of abusive actions (words or worse) on your part. Child abuse is becoming a major problem in this nation—so much so, that many communities are setting up free clinics in an attempt to help abusive parents.

With your children in mind, consider these Bible verses:

> Be devoted to one another in brotherly love; give preference to one another in honor; not lagging behind in diligence, fervent in spirit, serving the Lord (Rom. 12:10-11).

The demands of a child will keep you constantly aware of your spirit, your diligence, and your sincerity.

A TWENTY-YEAR PROCESS /

> Train up a child in the way he should go, even when he is old he will not depart from it (Prov. 22:6).

Guiding children *is* a long, hard, demanding responsibility. But so is any rewarding job. Expending the energy to interact with one another *is* part of living. Parenthood is a twenty-year-long haul, and it becomes the most

167

demanding when children are in their late teens.

PARENTHOOD IS A PARTNERSHIP /

Guiding children requires that parents set limits for their children, which not only demands working together to set limits, but also to administer them.

Thus, parenthood is a continuous, ongoing test of the marriage partnership. Not only must limits be set, but as a child or children grow older, they need to be adjusted. All of this requires good will and cooperation between parents.

PARENTHOOD TAKES ENERGY /

Interacting with people is tiring. There are good days and there are bad days. One day you have happy children. Another day it seems they are grumpy all day long.

Take a referee as an example of expending energy. He keeps the game going smoothly. He is expected to call the plays according to the limits, to be impartial, consistent, and cool-headed. His job can be tough or easy on any given day. It depends on the mood of the players, their skill, the importance of the game, even the weather. Some days there are few close calls and few penalties. Other days, there can be some debatable, close calls and many penalties.

He rises to the demands of the game. He is in on every play. The game requires more or less of his effort, but the limits don't change. And refereeing doesn't interfere with his personal fulfillment. It's part of it. He doesn't bemoan the fact that he isn't a spectator. He relishes the job.

Like refereeing, guiding children can be a tough job or an easy job on any given day. It depends on the mood of the children, who they are with, importance of the problems that come up, even the weather.

Some days all goes smoothly. No one is stepping over the limits or challenging the calls. Other days you blow the whistle constantly and are called upon to make some debatable decisions.

Guiding children isn't something that interferes with your personal life—it's part of life. The wholehearted parent doesn't bemoan the job. He or she relishes it.

Half the battle in parenthood is accepting the task

and the never-ending surprises and frustrations that keep coming up.

CONFIDENT EXPECTATION /

Setting limits and dealing with the inevitable resistance from the children to some of the limits is a real test of the marriage. There is either cooperation or competition over setting the limits and how to supervise them. The term *confident expectation* assumes that you are doing or requiring something you believe is worthwhile and in the best interests of your child. If you are, you will have enough conviction to see it through.

If parents are competitors rather than partners, they will likely have two sets of limits—one set when mother is home alone, another set when father is home alone.

The result? Bedlam. Or withdrawal of one of the parents from the discipline process.

The children will begin to play one parent against the other. One parent can hardly be *confidently expectant* when defying or contradicting the other parent.

You will either enjoy the job or it will irritate you. You either cooperate with your partner or you compete. You either diligently rise to the demands of the job, or you neglect it.

IT ALL WORKS TOGETHER /

You build your own self-respect or self-love as you cooperate with your partner in setting limits and administering them . . . as you remain loyal, cooperative, submissive, and committed unto death to do all in your power to guide your children into becoming wholesome, happy, contributing adults.

Again . . . the key to maintaining such a spirit demands a higher commitment:
As unto the Lord!

NOTE: The material in this chapter is adapted from the book, *I Want to Enjoy My Children* (Zondervan), by the same authors.

Conclusion

Conclusion

If your goal is to maintain good physical health you pay attention to some important details:

1. Diet
2. Sleep
3. Exercise

You need knowledge about these areas so you provide time and expend energy to inform yourself of what is involved. Your interest is to act according to your knowledge.

There may be days when you are tempted to, or even choose to consciously behave in ways contrary to your knowledge. Then you renew your commitment to your goal and start over again.

If, on a daily basis, you do what is necessary, you are on your way to good physical health. No one else can do these things for you.

Likewise, if your goal is to build self-respect—or self-love—you also pay attention to some important details.

You need knowledge, so you provide the time and energy to inform yourself of what is involved. Your intent is to act according to your knowledge. No one else can do this for you. Either you do this for yourself or it won't be done.

There may be days when you are tempted, or even choose to consciously behave in ways contrary to your knowledge. Then you renew your commitment to your goal and start over again.

If, on a daily basis, you act according to your

knowledge, you will build a healthy self-respect and will be in shape to love your neighbor.

If you neglect these areas you will sooner or later sense a dislike of yourself and your neighbor.

The Bible gives some broad, basic instructions for wholesome living:

Jesus said:

> You shall love the Lord your God with all your heart, and with all your soul, and with all your mind. This is the great and foremost commandment (Matt. 22:37-38).

How can you know if you love God that much? Jesus answers that question as He taught His disciples:

> If you love Me, you will keep My commandments (John 14:15).

That we can understand. If you seek physical health, you learn the fundamentals, get into shape, and strive constantly to stay in shape. The effort and the result is one of the delights of life.

If you seek self-respect—or self-love—you learn the fundamentals, get into shape, and strive constantly to stay in shape. The effort and the result is one of the delights of your life.

Jesus said there is a second commandment like the great and foremost one—and on these two commandments depend the "whole Law and the Prophets":

> You shall love your neighbor as yourself (Matt. 22:39).

I have spent a lifetime listening to the stories of people who don't like themselves. As a result, they have problems loving other people.

In short, if you don't love yourself, you are out of shape and unable to love your neighbor as Jesus commanded.

The details of why my clients don't love themselves vary, but gradually I've become aware of recurring themes in these stories as people tell me how they have chipped away at their own self-respect, which leads to personal anxiety and misery as well as trouble with other people. I repeat these once more:

1. Behavior
2. Speech
3. Reactions
4. Thoughts
5. Goals

To locate yourself—that is, to determine if your performance in each of these areas builds up or chips away at your self-respect—you need a standard to go by—a mirror. This book has used the Bible as the standard.

Hopefully, each chapter has whetted your appetite to know more, and you will search your Bible to enlarge your knowledge. I encourage you to review the chapters in this book again and again.

In recent years, I have observed rapid deterioration in marriages and families. It is for this reason that some brief comments and recommendations for further reading are included.

As your behavior, speech, reactions, thoughts, and goals come closer to matching God's commandments, you will have a growing sense of self-respect and a growing love for your neighbor—you are on the road to becoming indestructible.